Hidden Barriers
In The Setup

Hidden Barriers In The Setup

Sam Oputa

Contents

About the Author

———

RAISED IN AN ENVIRONMENT WHERE survival of the fittest is the norm, surviving becomes an art and sometimes, luck. Sam Oputa is as street smart as an average New Yorker. He has interests in American capitalism and politics. He is as politically smart as he is street smart.

He attended the City University of New York. He also received an MBA in 2005. Sam Oputa is also the author of the bestselling "Faith or Reason" and "Why Was Man Created?"

Visit Amazon's Sam Oputa Page:

http://www.amazon.com/Sam-Oputa/e/B00FUP8QEC/ref=dp_ byline_cont_pop_ebooks_1

Preface

———

5 Servants, be obedient to them that are your masters according to the flesh,
with fear and trembling, in singleness of your heart, as unto Christ.

Ephesians 6:5

THE BIBLE SOUNDED LIKE A tool right here. A tool for a bunch of slave masters. It sounded like a propaganda tool written by white slave masters intent on bringing some people to their knees while serving them. Only the slave masters could read and interpret the Bible for the slaves then, and they did a good job.

One thought many people had, especially slaves—white and black slaves—was the belief they picked up from the Holy Bible . . . that there is a heaven and a hell; thus, it was really "worth the while" to fully surrender their entire life to the slave masters because the Bible so admonished. The white slaves were privileged to buy back their freedom, but the black slaves had better believe in the Bible—or be sent to an untimely hell! It was a divide-and-conquer concept unwinding.

And thus, the slaves went with the masters' call for total submission of life in slavery. Today, even after slavery, the masters still make laws that guarantee a labor supply through incarceration. They must tell you how to live . . . or else. You are not even free to make your own decisions. How can you when economic power has been taken away from you? You can't seriously rebel against the laws because some will call for you to be shot or incarcerated.

The "masters" had reasoned with the slaves using the Bible. They forced the slaves to accept that there will be some incredible rewards in heaven for those who do good works for the slave master—the rich landowner—while living here on earth.

On one hand, the Bible was used to tell everyone that we were equal before God . . . while many were acquired as slaves. Oh yes, we are so equal—not on earth but in heaven.

The same slaves were admonished to serve their masters on earth because their reward is in heaven.

The Constitution of the United States borrowed the same concept. While the Constitution proclaims that all men are created equal, the Thirteenth Amendment, while abolishing slavery, was creating new prisoners of slaves. Today, the United States incarcerates more black people than anywhere else in the world.

The results of the divide-and-conquer practices were the old Jim Crow and the new Jim Crow laws of today. Perhaps you thought that Jim Crow was over.

When we have had people who took pride in racist remarks rise to positions of policy making, you wonder what kind of policies they would come up with now. Two such remarks came from a United States senator and are reproduced below.

"The Klan is needed today as never before, and I'm anxious to see its rebirth here in West Virginia and in every state in the nation."

"I shall never fight in the armed forces with a Negro by my side . . . Rather I should die a thousand times and see Old Glory trampled in the dirt, never to rise again, than to see this beloved

land of ours become degraded by race mongrels, a throwback to the blackest specimen from the wilds."

All you have to do is seek and you shall find the new Jim Crow. It is in plain sight: the hidden barriers in the setup.

It is mental slavery to hold and hang on to things that have stopped serving their intended purpose in a person's life. Thus, no people are more hopelessly enslaved than a people that falsely believe . . . that they are free.

CHAPTER 1

The Introduction

———

IMAGINE THE SETUP WHERE . . .

We profess to be a Christian nation, yet we are afraid of the pope. Just imagine that for a few seconds. Something is wrong. Very wrong. We say we are the freest nation on earth, yet we practice legislated racism and an under-the-carpet apartheid.

We proclaim that we are the greatest nation on earth, yet, we are scared to put all our human potential to use. We'd rather cage some of our human potential. We cage our people more than the rest of the world. We cage them as prisoners using trumped-up charges.

When we pretentiously announced to the world that they were free, we pulled the noose tighter on their freedoms using the exception in the Thirteenth Amendment.

Though we say they are free, we know that they have been caged permanently. We did something permanently stupid while we were temporarily upset with the fear of apprehension of what the slaves might do in the future.

Say what you will, you know the truth. The truth is—the system is set up to be racist in the United States in everything. The hidden barriers were in the setup.

Until we recognize that racism permeates the fabric of our society, we cannot even start to solve our problems.

The only thing standing between people of color and the economic meal of a lifetime is the systemic embroidery of racial laws into America's system of laws. Just like slavery, this was and is systemic and intentionally weaved into the fabric of the American way of life. Some still deny that racism exists. If it were possible, those same people would deny that slavery never happened.

It looks like the same racism/apartheid that pervades us can be found in faraway places too—like South Africa and Rhodesia—Northern and Southern, now Zambia, and Zimbabwe, while there is evidence that racism has subsided in places like Zambia, Zimbabwe, and South Africa. Racism has found ways to permeate the American society permanently. We were a racist nation from the beginning, and we still are. The structure for the country was hijacked and designed by a few huge landowners.

In Haiti, the landowners were dealt a blow—a very fatal blow—and the landowners in America took notice. The incident in Haiti was perhaps a clarion call for landowners in America to act. They learned they have to think protection and subjugation. It meant protection for the landowners and subjugation of the slaves before they rise up like what happened in Haiti. The landowners learned from Haiti to set up structures that would bring about protection of lives and properties of the landowners. They had to design a new society.

The result was legislation of systemic racism.

And very few understand the foundation of America except the doctored truth your teacher was made to teach you. When histories are written, they are always written from the perspective of the winner. As usual, the white landowners wrote a befitting history that would serve them for eternity, and they promoted such histories, and continue to promote it, to this day.

Is it not hypocritical how America's history carries on about freedom? It is either freedom of this or freedom of that. Our freedoms have names. There is the freedom of speech. There is the freedom of association. There is the freedom of worship. And then there is the freedom to possess guns. The right to keep and bear arms is the people's right to possess arms for their own defense. It was an English common law tradition, a longstanding common law right to keep and bear arms that was recognized before the creation of a written national constitution.

With all the swan song about these freedoms, are you not surprised that the people asked for the right to own guns to demand and enforce their God-given rights? The freedoms we claim are God given and so abundantly free; yet, we fought and continue to fight wars for our freedoms. Black folks in America are still fighting for freedoms. Are you surprised?

Freedom is your ability to do whatever you please, provided you do not infringe on other people's freedoms. If that is the true definition of freedom, then true freedom cannot be said to exist in some countries. We can even dare to say that freedoms described as God given have been taken away by landowners. It has become a token for bargaining.

We can also say that freedoms are legislated. The freedom to marry whoever you choose notwithstanding the sex has just been legislated (interpreted by the Supreme Court) in the United States. I heard some people say that this freedom is not God given. And you wonder what freedom is.

"We look forward to a world founded upon four essential human freedoms. The first is freedom of speech and expression—everywhere in the world. The second is freedom of every person to worship God in his own way—everywhere in the world. The third is freedom from want—everywhere in the world. The fourth is freedom from fear—anywhere in the world."
—President Franklin D. Roosevelt, Message to Congress, January 6, 1941

People have been programmed to think that if it is legal, it must be right. The system which encompasses the media programs you to think and believe that way. Legal does not mean it is good and right. Legality can be used to oppress. Legality can be used to kill and/or execute. Legality can be used to kosher what is bad and it becomes good . . . but is it right?

Slavery was once legal in many places many centuries ago. Sometimes, we should take a deep breath and ask—who or what determines what is legal? After answering this question for self, you start to see whether the country you live in practices rule of law for all or rule of law for a select few, and based on what criteria.

What if legality is used to amass privileges for one group and rob another group of privileges? Yet, they claim that they practice democracy of the people, by the people, and for the people.

We are still practicing a form of slavery. It is inequality explained away as freedom in semantics. Such semantics have hidden slavery in plain sight. Slavery was ended legally, but slavery is still alive. People just do not call anyone a slave today, but black folks are treated worse than slaves nowadays. When blacks and whites were considered property, they were treated better because they belonged to some rich, white landowner. They were simply property. That perhaps will shine a light as to the manner in which property and lives can be quantified in monetary terms in an instance of damage claims.

Have you noticed how some news organizations complain about the destruction of property and not human lives lost during uprisings? Perhaps they do this because such lives are nonwhite lives.

Some Americans are not ashamed of our past. Some of us want to relieve that past. And some of us are reliving that past, through various flags, monuments, and through the police.

This is how the *Merriam-Webster Dictionary* explains freedom:

1: The quality or state of being free: as

    a: the absence of necessity, coercion, or constraint in choice or action

    b: liberation from slavery or restraint or from the power of another: independence

    c: the quality or state of being exempt or released usually from something onerous <*freedom* from care>

    d: ease, facility <spoke the language with *freedom*>

    e: the quality of being frank, open, or outspoken <answered with *freedom*>

    f: improper familiarity

    g: boldness of conception or execution

    h: unrestricted use <gave him the *freedom* of their home>

2:

    a: a political right

    b: franchise, privilege

The fourth enumerated freedom by President Franklin D. Roosevelt is informative. We should like it. A lot too. It was as if he was looking African Americans in the eye when he crafted that one.

Since 1941 when he spoke those words, African Americans have also crafted a slogan—*black lives matter*, 64 years later. What went wrong? Why is there a need in God's own country for its citizens to be crying out loudly using such slogans as *blacklivesmatter*?

Where are the freedoms?

There are three levels of class created in those days and over the years. The first class are the rich white men who were the landowners. The very few owned the largest lands in America. They needed people to till the land. There were no people to till the land. They needed people to provide protection, and there were not enough people—black or white.

Solution: Bring in shiploads of convicted murderers of European lineage and auction them off in the New World. They were sold off—men, women, and children.

Later, those with long sentences joined the group of white slaves. They were the first group of slaves. They were all-white slaves. If you did not dig into history, you would not know that white folks were slaves first. It is as if it is an unspoken culture. If anyone, black or white, thinks and/or is of the assumption that slavery was only an African experience, then you have been misinformed. That assumption is completely wrong. Irish slavery and African slavery are a subject worth remembering along the same lines and is not worth erasing from our memories.

The Irish slave trade began when James II sold about 30,000 Irish prisoners as slaves to the New Found Lands. He made a proclamation in 1625 that required Irish political prisoners to be sent to the New World and sold to English settlers in the West Indies/Caribbean. By the 1650s, the Irish were the main slaves sold to Antigua and Montserrat.

There were so many Irish slaves at that time, that 70 percent of the total population of Montserrat were Irish slaves. It is therefore extremely important to understand this part of history because it will explain the success of capitalism and racism, as we shall see later. If you don't grasp this, the purpose of this book to understanding—the *Hidden Barriers in the Setup*—will be lost.

Ireland, at the beginning, was the biggest source of slaves for English merchants. The majority of the first slaves to the New World were actually white.

Beginning in 1641 and up to 1652, more than 500,000 Irish were killed by the English and 300,000 more were sold as slaves. It was so bad that Ireland's population was diminished by more than a half. It fell from approximately 1,500,000 to 600,000 in just a decade.

You may have learned about the African slavery and the gory details—the lynching, public display of hanging bodies, killings, etc. Well, *all* the slaves suffered the same fate. All slaves were simply property.

Whenever the white slaves rebelled or disobeyed an order, they were punished in the harshest of ways. Slave owners who are the landowners would hang their human property by their hands or feet. Sometimes they would hang by their hands while the feet were set on fire as a form of punishment.

Sometimes they were simply burned alive . . . or shot. It was accepted practice to have their cut-off heads placed on pikes in a public place as a warning to other slaves—black or white.

It was because the white slaves were insufficient, could not cope, and were not as productive as desired, that the need arose for new slaves.

White or black, slaves were poor and badly treated. They were the lowest class of society. They could be shot at impulse and discarded with—no questions asked—they were simply property. They were the property of the rich landowner. The landowner did not care whether the slave was white or black. All the landowner cared about was that they carried out their orders.

However, following the incident in Haiti where landowners were suddenly attacked and eliminated by the slaves, an urgency arose to change modus operandi. The concept of divide and conquer was implemented immediately.

This is not the only time such practices were employed. They were also found in the Bible, Quran, and some other so-called holy books. The books were handed to Africans while white men and Arabs plundered the gold and human resources in exchange.

There happens to be evidence that such was the modus operandi of the landowners who mostly were rich, white, and men. Just like they operated in America, so they operated in Australia too.

Australia was also populated by criminals sent from Europe. Now, these poor white European criminals-turned-slaves constituted another class when their services were needed.

The demand for manpower increased. To fill this need, Africa became the destination for human resources. When the African slaves first arrived, they were on the same footing as their white counterparts from Europe until they—the black slaves—were legislated out of the emerging freedoms. They could not: 1. buy or work their way out of slavery and 2. could be hanged or shot by their owners as part of their punishment.

And their white counterparts were enticed with some freedoms like:

1. They could work their way out of slavery
2. Killing was removed as part of their punishment

Thus, the foundation for capitalism was laid, and the foundation for racism had just been laid. The foundation for early policing had just been laid. The foundation of a polarized society had been laid.

The word to watch is *legislation,* and some legislated laws are still haunting some citizens of God's own country to this day. Through legislation, we have, intentionally, or unintentionally, legislated three groups of people classified as:

1. The rich white man
2. The poor white slave who had a path to freedom
3. The black slave who had no path to freedom

In today's jargon, the above classification is still the norm but dressed in beautiful spin words such as:

1. The 10 percent
2. The middle class
3. And the rest—the poor

You can assign your spin words as:

a. Rich
b. Middle class and
c. Poor, or some other way as:
    1. Corporations
    2. Middle class and
    3. Poor

While the 10 percent takes home nearly 76 percent of all the income, the poor and the middle class who make up 90 percent of the population take home the remaining 24 percent income. *Credit Suisse Global Wealth Databook* finds that in the U.S., 75.4 percent of all wealth is owned by the richest 10 percent of the people. This was a 2013 report.

It gets worse.

The not-so-funny part is that the rich are still having it their way. They can buy everybody, or, are most people not already working for them in the present-day big farms and corporations? You may think you are not, but that is a subject for another day.

How do they do this, you might ask. In the days of slavery, they bought and sold the poor. It was at their behest that the middle class was created.

Remember, the middle class came from the white slaves. The rich landowners traded freedom for protection from slaves by smartly forcing the mostly Irish white slaves to buy themselves off. The newly freed slaves saw it as a good trade-off.

P.S.: Check who had the largest population in your local police force in the 1950s. Today, who are mostly hired in the coercion agencies you know of? Why is it so?

Remember, the middle class were slaves who were granted freedom/amnesty to accumulate some resources. If the rich men decided that they wanted to eliminate the middle class, they could legislate it. If you really think about it, both the middle class and the poor in the United States share less than 25 percent of the total wealth. So, what is so "middle class" about middle class?

Another not-so-funny thing is that the middle class has suddenly forgotten history. History tells us that the middle class was the creation of the rich men and for a purpose. History tells us that the middle class were slaves and in the clutches of slavery not too long ago. Is it not funny how the well fed tend to think that the beggar is lazy?

The rich did not get rich by being stupid. That, we must give them. The rich are not ready to give up their riches. The rich will do whatever it takes to stay rich—whether through guns, cutlasses, spears, or by bows and arrows.

But among other considerations, safety is uppermost in the rich man's mind. The 10 percent understands more than anyone else that he must have stability to enjoy the wealth.

That is the single most important reason why he transformed the white slaves. He transformed the white slaves to serve as his police for his protection.

One of the reasons for setting up the police department in the South was to capture runaway slaves and to put down any uprisings.

Can you imagine if those white slaves were not given some freedoms? Can you imagine if there was no middle class? It was a ploy. It is called *divide and conquer*. Give them a little freedom and the white slaves would believe they got it a little bit better than their black counterparts.

Though there was the middle class that had its origins from white slaves being able to pay off their masters and be free and earn some resources, not all of them were able to do just that. There were many poor white folks. The poor white folks and their black counterparts were not forgotten. They were not forgotten to die while hungry. They were given a little to feed on but not to feed fat.

Today, with campaign contributions, it is very simple to manipulate everything, including legislation, if you have the resources. There are always elements available to you to ma nipulate to achieve your objective.

CHAPTER 2

Understanding America's Racism

WHITE SUPREMACY IS A SYSTEMIC, institutionally perpetuated system of exploitation of continents, nations of peoples, specifically peoples of color, by a few rich white peoples from nations of the European continent, for the purposes of maintaining power for the acquisition of wealth and privilege. The watchwords are *rich white men*. Ask yourself . . . Is anything wrong with this? Is this not normal human behavior? Was this type of behavior not found in empires far removed from Europe? As you ponder on those questions, let us explain, point-by-point, why such behavior is systemic and far more pronounced in the United States.

WHAT DOES IT MEAN WHEN PEOPLE SAY IT IS THE SYSTEM OR SYSTEMIC?

One of the common mistakes people make when they talk about racism is to believe that it is a collection of prejudices and random individual acts of discrimination. They do not know, understand, or see systemic racism because it is so subtle. Day in, day out, you hear the part in the National Anthem that goes thus: ". . . the land of the free, and home of the brave." You say to self—this is the land of the free and home of the brave.

Most people cannot even fathom, see, or understand the systemic culture and its implementation. They do not see that it is in the system. Yet, we all live it—some more than the others. Some of us do not see the web of interlocking reinforcements through institutional structures—in the economic, military, legal, educational, religious, and culture that gave rise to racism. Such institutional structures also give teeth to racism.

Some do not see or perhaps pretend to not observe in most institutions, a systemic reinforcement of racism in the police, Congress, political parties (Democrats and Republicans), and the presidency.

As a system, racism affects your every aspect of life in this country, and, pathetically, most blacks cannot even see it, and where they see it, they must learn to live with it. Because a few people of color see the purchase of a Dunkin' Donut or a McDonald's franchise as "success stories," such delusions of success positions them not to see that racism is systemic. The mistake is: They tend to personalize racism and racist acts.

They start to see any act of racism as an aberration rather than the norm. One wonders why they cannot see the tokenism in the piecemeal acquisition of a Burger King franchise as an aberration and not the norm. Perhaps such franchise practices are the attempt to meet the quota of affirmative action.

When policing in the heavily populated city neighborhoods becomes a shoot-before-you-aim, when police shoot first and ask questions later, when policing becomes shoot first for any reason—or no reason—because police can talk their way out of such shootings, then you start to wonder why most, if not all, the police shootings and killings are mostly taking place in big cities.

Many do not know that current practices of institutionalized racism have roots in the formation of capitalism—and African Americans were to be prevented from participating in this capitalism.

White slaves were granted amnesty to buy back their freedoms and therefore were eligible to amass wealth. Black slave labor was exploited to build the American capitalism—capitalism they were forbidden to participate in.

Common sense would have it that in order to maintain the systems of racism and capitalism, the landowners must, as a matter of necessity, maintain a network of coercive structures necessary for enforcement of any goal then or in the future.

These structures include the police and many other policelike structured organizations. Sometimes you wonder if the intention for maintaining such coercive might, including mass surveillance and mass incarceration, were not just to police the societies but to cage some of the people, especially in neighborhoods where nonwhites are quarantined.

This is why the term *White Supremacy* is more meaningful than the raggedy ascription of racism. Racism is beyond hate. It is beyond prejudice. What does it matter to you if somebody hates you? It takes no money from your pocket. What does it matter if someone is prejudiced against you? It does not take your life away.

When the hate and prejudice is backed by the taking away of privileges and other freedoms, then your way of life is affectively controlled and quarantined. It is then systemic.

The term *racism* is not systemic by itself. It has no effect on its own, though it is affective. There must be an actionable goal and enforcement to make it systemic.

Thus, white supremacy, if it exists and by its goals, if any, is nothing new or bad because other tribes ascribe to ethnocentricity and domination of others. Where such practices become evil in modern times is when it starts to set parameters for who should or should not participate in the capitalism originally built by all—especially by those whose sweat watered the cultivated lands. To then sideline such a group by systemic racial maneuverings speaks of a campaign that has lost its ethical moorings.

Whites get to have lower incarceration rates because their neighborhoods are not targeted for overpolicing. Also, laws are not unfairly written to make sure they do time—and more of it.

FIG 1

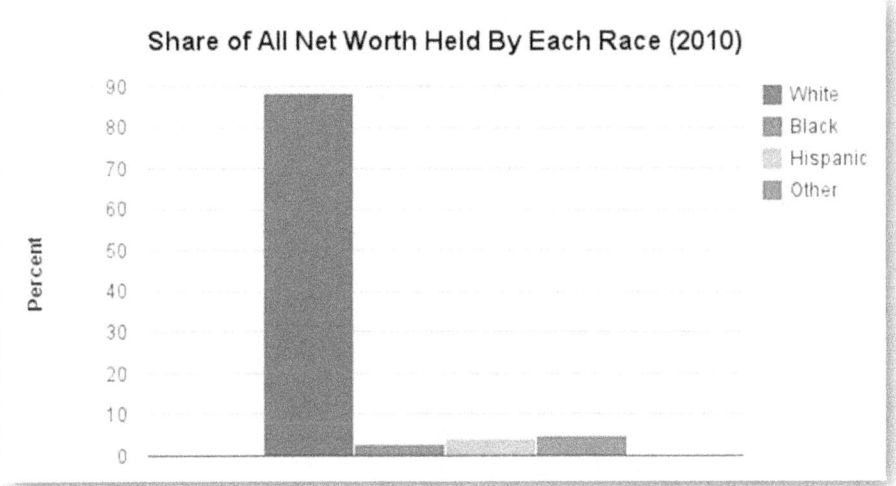

Whites are much wealthier as a group than they would have been if they didn't steal land and use the free labor of enslaved black people for their benefit. Today's financial success of America and the West is directly and indirectly linked to the institution of slavery.

When people use the term *racism*, it often leads to dead-end debates. Debates centered on hate and prejudice which most often are hard to put one's hands on. In such debates, the real issues are usually unknown and difficult to see. It becomes just "them against us." The real issues in such situations are thus sidestepped.

A clearer picture of racism (white supremacy) could be painted if we analyze how a certain action relates to the systemic culture of white supremacy.

White supremacy is the theory, belief, or doctrine that white people are inherently superior to people from all other racial groups and are therefore, rightfully, the dominant group in any society. That definition also summarizes, in a nutshell, racism. It has no affect until it is actionable.

Most people use the term *white supremacy* for white people as the clear choice of a people supporting and implementing a system that gives them privilege.

Always bear in mind that America was founded on capitalism. Capitalism, among other things, thrives and will only thrive where there is competition. If you take out competition, capitalism will die. Now, remember that whenever you hear the narratives about the reason(s) for the American Civil War.

Some narratives say America went to war because the big government was after states' rights. Another narrative says that the war was fought to free the slaves. If you believe the second narrative, you will believe anything. Thus, you believe that suddenly, the white man woke up one morning and decided to go to war and spill his "superior" blood for the "inferior" blood of the slaves, right?

Let us also consider why America went to war with Iraq. This happened in the not-so-distant past, yet people have various narratives as reason(s) for the war. One narrative says it was all about the oil. Another narrative has it that it was all about weapons of mass destruction—WMD.

The WMD narrative would have stuck if politics had not descended to the nasty level it has at this moment. What do you think? For you to make a good call as to the reason for the Iraqi war, you have to know the agenda of those making the decisions—neocons and whoever they were taking marching orders from who else but—the rich landowners. I have not seen or read of any rationale for wars of such magnitude without economic ramifications.

A common explanation was that the Civil War was over the moral issues of slavery. Some historians write that the Civil War was over the institution of slavery and much more.

Indeed, it was the economics of slavery and political control of that system that was central to the conflict. It was a war over capitalism fought by capitalists on opposing sides. It was purely economic.

Arguments on moral issues of slavery cannot be true; after all, arguments discounting morality and justifying slavery had been carved into the same holy book used to manipulate the minds of the slaves. The fact that slavery exists in the Bible is no secret. There were laws in the Bible regulating the practice of slavery: how to buy, sell, free, or punish slaves.

Any and all other narratives are semantics intended to butter the nasty side of capitalism and lessen the ugly level of perceived ethical moorings.

CHAPTER 3

Explaining White Supremacy

THIS IS NOT ABOUT DISSECTING white supremacy. It is just a simple explanation of it. When historians write the early history of America, they tend to start from a convenient beginning while ignoring or making less of a fuss about the inconvenient past.

They sometimes write as if they are writing on behalf of the conquerors who had issued a threat of—or else. If you read history from their perspectives, what you get is not history but doctored story lines meant to uplift immoral acts and lies into heroic truths.

I'll give you one right here. That Christopher Columbus discovered America is just one lie out of many in all imaginable reasoning perspectives and ramifications. Christopher may have discovered America for the Europeans but not for the inhabitants of the land. Not even for the Chinese explorers who may have visited the land many times before Christopher Columbus was even born.

Some white historians just love to turn lies into facts. It's as if they are under the command of a general or king. Somehow, they write lies and expect the lies to have supremacy over the truths. The lies were widespread, and they were accepted.

Let it be reiterated that if you want to get the true facts of history, you must read from the perspectives of both the winner and vanquished, and in between lies the truth. If you read ancient history only from the white man's perspective, you will soon start to accept some falsehoods like the one that portrays Africa as a smaller continent than she really is.

Every nation supposedly has a creation myth, which, of course, is the story that the people are taught. It the story of how the nation came into being. For some nations, the myth has been torn down or changed and sometimes borrowed and implemented in faraway places.

American history began with Christopher Columbus's "discovery" of America. Then the Pilgrims came to settle. The stories of how the white pilgrims suffered will be narrated for the empathetic ears. Thus, the history tellers went on to tell the story of how America won her independence from England, the American Revolution, and then expanded westward until it became the enormous country it is today—a land from sea to shining sea.

That is how some white historians tell the story. When the Indians tell the story, it is different while bringing in new perspectives. And when the slaves told their stories, you find that some history books were written from a different perspective purposely so much so, that they left out some material events. The omitted key facts about the birth and growth of America as a nation makes you understand the phrase "truth is relative."

The facts also demonstrate that white supremacy was fundamental to the existence of the United States of America.

Today, does it worry you when you hear slogans such as: Let us take our country back? What does it remind you of? Truthfully!

The United States is a nation created by military conquest by Europeans seeking continental wealth. It was conquered in installments.

The plan was to annihilate the peoples of the lands and then seize the lands inhabited by the "Indian" nations. The indigenous peoples were nicknamed *Indians*. Was this really new? It has always been part of human existence from the times of the gods. The Bible would confirm such behaviors from time. However, one wonders who were the authors of the books that made up the Bible. Yes—the Bible!

Prior to the European invasion, there existed indigenous people who were later nicknamed Indians because Christopher Columbus thought he was in India. Why he thought he was in India baffles the mind. It is estimated that the New World had approximately 9 to 18 million indigenous people.

By the end of the Indian/European wars to retain and take over the land, there were about 250,000 indigenous people left in what is now the United States of America. In the north in what is now Canada, about 123,000 indigenes were left standing according to Annette Jaimes in the book—*The State of Native America: Genocide, Colonization, and Resistance* (Race & Resistance Series).

Today, if any group does this type of behavior, that group will be accused of genocide, and that was exactly what the Europeans did. Thus, the massacre of indigenous landowners was the first prerequisite for the establishment of the United States.

The second prerequisite was the procurement of slaves. This is very important. We have to separate the slaves into white and Africans. It is very important in that the future of America and the creation of hierarchy of classes will mirror these—the owners, white slaves, and African slaves.

The United States could not have been economically developed in a short period of time as a nation without slave labor—African and white. However, it was the African slaves that provided the engine that powered the economic engine at the time.

These days, some misinformed people love to liken African Americans as being lazy. African slaves were not likened to laziness then when the economic well-being of the United States depended on them. In fact, at the time, landowners were budgeting over 75 pounds sterling for a black male slave, and that was the average asking price. Irish slaves fetched an average of only 5 pounds sterling. Seventy-five pounds in the year 1705, in today's value, is over $17,540.34

The more the agricultural activities expanded, the more the African slaves were imported to meet demand. At one point, not enough white slaves came from Europe, and the European invaders did not have enough indigenous peoples to put to work in sufficient numbers because the invaders had decimated the population. Thus, the abundance of enslaved Africans provided the labor force that spurred the economic growth and sometimes growth in technological innovation in the geographical landmass of what we now refer to as the United States of America.

Another move in putting together the country—USA—was wars, or threat of wars. Recall that the United States had already taken part of Mexico. Today, we call that part Texas, and made it the state of Texas in 1845.

Soon, another territory of Mexico would be seized under the 1848 Treaty of Guadalupe Hidalgo. A few years later, in 1853, the U.S. acquired a final chunk of Arizona from Mexico by threatening to renew the war. This completed the territorial boundaries of what is now the United States. Those were the three foundational stones of the United States as a nation.

Remember that a mistake repeated more than once becomes the modus operandi. It is no longer a mistake. So, if you were thinking that the Europeans made a mistake in the conscious decisions to use force to acquire what was needed, you have not started thinking at all. And the operations on that line took a decisive key step in 1898, with the takeover of Puerto Rico, Guam, the Philippines, and Cuba through the route of war—that is, the Spanish-American War.

All the aforementioned colonies except Cuba have remained as U.S. colonies, providing additional wealth and military bases for the United States. Thus, all the above including the 1898 takeover completed the acquisition of lands that ultimately formed the United States of America.

These same modus operandi were not limited to forming the United States. They were used in some other continents like Australia and Africa. Most historians will not tell you like it was. They cook the truth to a level where it sounds nice and heroic to the ears. Some make heroes of murderers. It depends on who or whose side the historian is on.

The foundation of racism was laid when American capitalism became a concept in exploitation. The roots of racism and discrimination were a cry for protection by the landowners when they, out of fear and concern of what had happened in Haiti (the slave revolution), established economic exploitation by the theft of resources and human labor—white and black.

The Haitian Revolution was a successful antislavery insurrection that shook the former French colony of Saint Domingue from 1791 and lasted till 1804. As the revolution took hold and ultimately succeeded, the landowners in the United States were watching and learning. Understanding this particular event will lead you to a clearer understanding that it was a defining moment in the racial histories of the Americas.

One of the legacies of the Haiti Revolution was the demolition of long-held beliefs about black inferiority. It brought to the fore the enslaved peoples' hunger for freedom and the capacity to achieve and maintain freedom. The slaves' organizational capacity and abilities shocked the Americas and especially frightened the landowners and slave owners in the United States.

This event led the landowners to the divide-and-conquer concept to vanquish the slaves who were white and black. Thus, the landowners established a racist capitalism where whites were allowed to participate, and the blacks kept out, even though the blacks were the fuel for capitalism.

The white slaves thus served as the coercive and security arm of the landowners. It is still that way today.

That fear led to a justification that exploitation by institutionalizing inferiority of its citizens was good for capitalism.

The application of racism by the landowners was against all non-white peoples. It was clear-cut—whites vs nonwhites.

One can argue that racism and economic power go hand in hand. One can also argue that capitalism is racist. It should be. It was created by racism through racism for greedy landowners. Notice that the description of the landowners was . . . *greedy landowners*, not racist landowners. If the system is not racist, why were black people deliberately and systemically left out? Let's use the same chart and paragraph on an earlier page again to make this illustration.

Whites have lower incarceration rates because their neighborhoods are not targeted for overpolicing. Also, laws are not unfairly written to make sure they do time—and more of it. Refer to FIG 1

Whites are much wealthier as a group than they would have been if they didn't steal land and use the free labor of enslaved black people for their benefit. Today's financial success of America and the West is directly and indirectly linked to the institution of slavery.

THE CRIMINALIZATION OF BLACK LIVES IN THE UNITED STATES

Why do you think that a law was fashioned after the British trespass law to protect properties and trespassing? Let us be reasonable while answering this question in our minds. When you create monsters of a group of people, do you wonder why people arm themselves to defend against the monsters?

It just seems like they can make of black people anything they wish. They can make slaves out of blacks. They can make blacks poor. They can stop them from participating in American capitalism. They can legislate out black people from all economic activities that benefit black folks.

They can also criminalize blacks so that they can be locked up, reduced in numbers, brutalized, and shot. If you cannot see it, it is because the laws that criminalize nonwhites are the hidden barriers in the setup.

Those in power knew they could use drugs as a weapon of oppression and destabilization of communities. There were those who employed drugs to brand and criminalize the hippies and people of color. It is still done today. In those days, they associated marijuana and heroin with hippies and black communities.

Those in charge, through the media, did a good job of getting the public to associate hippies with marijuana. They even did a better job at getting the media to criminalize and associate blacks with heroin, marijuana, and other narcotics. What followed then was that criminalizing the unwanted groups made it easy to disrupt those communities.

You see, when you want to kill a dog, you say it is a mad dog with rabies. The landowners understand this more than anyone, and, yes, they own the media too.

Thus, the authorities could arrest black leaders and the ordinary retail street drug dealer, raid their homes, break up their protests, and vilify them night and day on the news. This used to be the best excuse to overpolice a community. Black communities got their overdose of overpolicing.

It was like adding gammalin 20 to a lake and wait for the fish to come floating up. Police became fishers of black men and women. It was like the slave days in the South. And they caught a lot of fish. They depleted the lake, which was, of course, the original plan to fill the jails—the New York Stock Exchange listed jails with raw materials.

Of course, white folks have a lower incarceration rate. Their neighborhoods are not and would not be targeted for overpolicing. Where do you think the police officers live? Meanwhile, the laws are not written in such a way to give wiggle room to judges (who are mostly white) to use discretion but to make sure nonwhites do time—and more of it.

RONALD REAGAN AND THE H. W. BUSH YEARS

Those years were perhaps some of the worst years for black folks out of the slavery years. Black folks in those years were not even allowed to live peacefully in poverty as usual. They had to be destabilized, jailed, or killed—whichever came first.

The so-called war on drugs was nothing more than a population control method through drugs.

They were the years the black communities were fully pumped full of illegal drugs. The ploy to deplete and destroy the black communities was a full-blown war. Whether by arrests, convictions, drug territory wars, murders, fires, or robberies, whole communities were devastated.

The majority of the arrestees were nonwhites. The murders were black-on-black. The convictions were mostly blacks. Those who planned the devastation were enjoying a huge success.

And they dubbed it—*war on drugs*, or better still—*just say no to drugs*. Did you ever wonder how the drugs were getting into the country and straight into the black neighborhoods? The black folks were/

are being played like a fiddle, and they, the black folks, produced every tune requested.

BILL CLINTON YEARS

The Bill Clinton years did not make matters better. The black neighborhoods, perhaps, felt a little relief initially. The three-strikes-you-are-out crime bill was introduced. It was the 1990s. Half the states and the federal government had enacted mandatory sentencing laws for repeat crime offenders.

The enactment of the mandatory sentencing laws created a harvest of raw materials for the private correctional facilities. The harvests were mostly nonwhites.

It is no longer news that the United States has the highest incarceration rate in the World. This is deliberate because those being incarcerated in large numbers are blacks. It did not just begin today. It began in the era when the landowners deliberately paved a way to free white slaves while tightening the ropes on the necks of black people. The fear of black revenge that led the landowners to make policy mistakes is the same fear guiding today's policy makers to strengthen the hidden barriers in the setup . . . by any means.

When you do an analysis of President Clinton's crime bill and bills like it, you will be led to a larger understanding of black America's historical bridge to nowhere in the United States, and a frightening understanding of how that history has woven into the fabric of present-day realities.

If you were invited to a TV talk show to discuss crime and you did your research well, your analysis will definitely say that under the administrations of Reagan and Clinton, mass incarcerations of minorities—a social tool used for punishment—also became a major job creator with succulent salaries. All you have to do is have an open mind to study the plights of a people.

This topic will be given special attention in a subsequent chapter, but for starters, below are a few provisions of the 1994 crime bill.

The 1994 crime bill cost $30 billion that helped to accelerate the growth of the prison industrial complex. Some of the provisions, which compared to a declaration of war, include:

a. $10.8 billion in federal funds to assist local governments nationwide to hire 100,000 new police officers over 5 years.
b. $10 billion for new federal prisons.
c. An increase in the number of federal crimes to which the death penalty applied. It grew from two to 58.
d. In an instance, the bill eliminated an already existing statute that prohibited the execution of mentally incapacitated defendants.
e. The main provision of the three-strikes proposal which mandated life sentences for persons convicted of three "violent" felonies. The definition of violent perhaps is not color blind.
f. A section that allowed children as young as 13 to be tried as adults—ridiculous.

With the above provisions (and there were more), the traps were set for the peoples who had been prepped for failure from time through all the systemic racist laws. Now was time to finish them off.

Just imagine for a moment if the billions spent was invested on the people *before* they became prisoners. It is as if it was better to destroy these lives because they were mostly black lives. Meanwhile, it must be said that black leaders were privy to the crime bill. If President Clinton did not have the hindsight, neither did the black leaders.

FIG 2

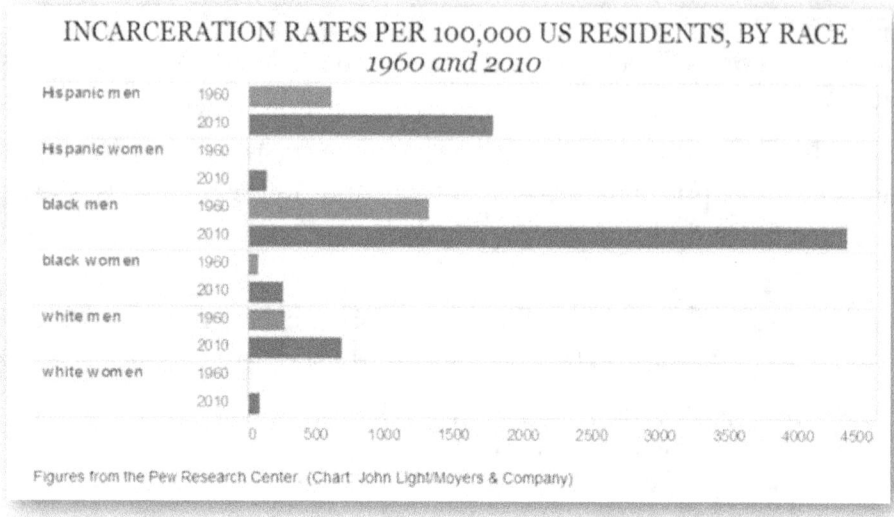

Whites have lower incarceration rates because their neighborhoods are not targeted for overpolicing. Also, laws are not unfairly written to make sure they do time—and more of it.

STILL ON DEMONIZING BLACK PEOPLE

During slavery, the skills of some of the slaves were far well above those of the slave owners. Their skills were so good, they were inventing one thing here and another thing there. Today, the history books have it that Eli Whitney invented and patented the cotton gin in 1793.

Of course, Eli Whitney can claim that; after all, the slaves that designed the idea were considered his property. Property, as it were, belonged to the owners, and thus, any idea from the slaves belonged to the owner.

The grand irony was that the person who provided Eli Whitney with the key idea that resulted into a patent was himself a slave, known to us only by the one name Sam. Sam's father had solved the critical problem of removing seeds from cotton by developing a kind of comb to do the job. Whitney's cotton gin only went further to simply mechanize the idea of this comb.

In other words, most of the technological ideas during the slave era flowed from the slaves; after all, they were the people who were doing the jobs in the fields. They were better positioned to come up with good ideas. The story of Sam is just one. There were many others that were repeated in different ways over and over. Slaves invented technological ideas, but since slaves were property, the masters patented the ideas as their own. Thus, our knowledge of slave contributions comes to us in anecdotal forms.

The point of the above is to draw your attention to the skills of the slaves. They can compete. They were ready for the job market if they became freed.

But no sooner were they freed than unions were formed. The purpose of those unions was to secure the emerging jobs for the white populace. If you are not in the unions, you cannot get the jobs. And the unions were not allowed to admit nonwhites. The attempt to stifle nonwhites was preplanned and thus, permeated the American society.

The problems for the freed black slaves had just started. To this day, that trend has not abated. When you cannot have a job or any other way to support life, what can you do?

Perhaps one way was to crawl back to your masters and beg for a job at any price the masters deemed right. But the price cannot be right for the slave.

Mostly homeless with a box containing only a few possessions, freedmen fleeing to Union lines for jobs found themselves rejected for any jobs whatsoever. They therefore found themselves dependent on the federal government for their existence as they had been on their masters.

Has that sort of dependency on government been broken yet? Or, is such dependence promoted as a means to an end today?

Even the federal authorities had no concrete policy concerning the welfare of the freedmen. Therefore, those charged with their welfare resorted to various means of providing them with food, shelter, and clothing. To this day, the poor are still receiving food, shelter, and clothing. They are receiving such not because they are lazy but because that is how the system is set up. It is systemic. Do you think that people, any people, would prefer hand-to-mouth economic existence to being in the middle or rich class?

Perhaps an article from CivilWarTalk.com described it best in these words:

> *Many freedmen, herded into contraband camps, were hired out to loyal Unionist plantation owners for low wages, and others in the Western theater were assigned parcels of confiscated lands for subsistence farming. Still others rendered service to the army.*
>
> *Unaccustomed to administering refugee relief, the army generally managed to maintain freedmen at a subsistence level. But many died of disease in overcrowded stockades, and some voluntarily returned to their homes because of deplorable conditions. Supplemental aid arrived from Northern relief societies that collected food and clothing for the freedmen and by 1862 began sending teachers to educate them. That year, the New England Freedman's Aid Society was operating schools in South Carolina, and before war's end, blacks in Mississippi and Georgia had founded schools for their own people.*
>
> *Not all freedmen dared trust whites professing friendship. Abuses of slavery were fresh in their minds, and many suffered injustices at the hands of invading white soldiers. Knowing the war was not over, unsure of what or whom to believe, many preferred to stay with their masters, whose power over them would remain after Union forces moved on. Others joined the Federal army after 1863, or followed it aimlessly, not knowing what else to do.*

CHAPTER 4

Racism and Capitalism

───────

CAPITALISM IS A GOOD THING. Greed is also a good thing. The degree of exploitation at which both are practiced becomes the issue. Racism is bad at any level. Racism hurts the practice and good name of capitalism.

The United States was the first nation to introduce racism. It was also the first to initiate capitalism; thus, racism was a means to capitalism. As the research for this chapter was going on, it was no surprise to find that a great deal of work has been done on this topic. It was as if the authors and I had the same thought processes. Some of the works argued that without slavery there would be no capitalism.

Perhaps that was true then but obviously not true today. Some argued that slavery was the fuel for capitalism. Perhaps that was true then. It is partially true if you consider the wages some workers get today, especially in the farming sector. It was noticed that nowhere was there such a trend in the debate on capitalism more than it is in the United States. Sometimes the debates take the form of workers' walkout from the job and other protestations.

Perhaps, some of us have done some scholarly student homework during our college days on capitalism, but nothing we had written in college homework mimicked our thought processes today as grown and highly experienced professionals.

We have also read the various reasons for the Civil War from different historians with different perspectives. The understanding of the workings of capitalism/racism during its inception and infancy makes the true reason for the Civil War pop out at you with no reasonable doubt.

There was no way the landowners, though of two differing sides, were going to sacrifice their superior "pure" white blood to free the inferior "impure" black slaves.

The real reason for the Civil War, like most other wars, is simply economic. It was not a war fought for the freedom of slaves. It was a war fought for a level playing field for the capitalists.

If the war was for the equality of all Americans, then that was a lost war because black folks are not truly as free as freedom dictates. And why are black folks still on the streets marching for their freedom? Blacks are today enjoying freedom—the freedom on paper, *not* freedom to participate in America's capitalism. They were excluded before the Civil War. They are excluded to this day by hidden barriers in the setup.

Merriam-Webster's Dictionary defines *racism* as
: poor treatment of or violence against people because of their race or
: the belief that some races of people are better than others

Racism can also be defined as
: a belief that race is the primary determinant of human traits and capacities and that racial differences produce an inherent superiority of a particular race
: racial prejudice or discrimination

The Anti-Defamation League defines *racism* as the hatred of one person by another—or the belief that another person is less than human . . .

while,

Wikipedia says of it—racism consists of ideologies and practices that seek to justify, or cause, the unequal distribution of privileges, rights, or goods among different racial groups.

Of all the three definitions above, perhaps, Wikipedia's best describes American society. For the purposes of this book, Wikipedia's definition best captures the sentiments. It captured some my thoughts. I especially like the use of the words "*. . . the unequal distribution of privileges.*"

Privileges took the place of the word *freedom*. Like freedoms, privileges can also be legislated.

In our households, when the husband and wife work, they bring in more resources. That is a fact. The rent is one and thus, cheaper for the household. When all the family is home and a lightbulb is turned on, it is one bulb for all. It is one electric bill, one water bill, and one mortgage/rent payment.

Thus, such a household is likely to have savings as both parents are firing on both cylinders, so to speak. And soon, the need for food and shelter are met.

Abraham Maslow's Hierarchy of Needs explained it well. When an individual cannot feed or clothe self, his thoughts cannot go beyond the thought of food. It does not matter your background.

When an individual has no freedoms or is denied privileges that are easily available to others, their thoughts cannot exceed that of slaves. Slaves had no hope. So, why must they think for self? If they planned, they planned for the landowner. If they had any thoughts whatsoever, it must be how to please "master" so that the individual's life would not be in jeopardy.

What Abraham Maslow said is so right that every day you can see that simple concept in the daily lives of individuals, peoples, and nations. America can think big. America can think of exploring the universe. Developing nations cannot. Developing nations are preoccupied thinking about how to build their democracies, roads, and infrastructures. By the way, that developing nations are busy thinking of stable democracies is because the white man's ways of life were forced down their throat. Some white governments still think (and wrongly too) that they can force their type of democracy down the throat of other nations today.

Is it not ironic that while Great Britain and Europe were busy dismantling kingdoms and kings for democracy, they were busy propping and glorifying their own kings/queens, even to this day?

The developing nations had no choice but to dump their way of life for the white man's. Abraham Maslow opined that humans are motivated by some basic (or deficiency) needs (e.g., physiological, safety, love, and esteem) and growth needs that lead to self-actualization.

It is evident that the landowners had many intentions for the slaves, but self-actualization was *not* one of them. There was no freedom. Perhaps the only freedom the slaves enjoyed was to stay alive to carry out the masters' orders. Even after their so-called freedom, nonwhites were kept away from any privileges so much so, that such a huge population was barred from participating in the emerging capitalism.

In some countries, women are not allowed to work or even drive. Women make up approximately 51 percent of most countries' population. For the United States, of the 316,497,531 individuals, 50.85 percent are women. Can you think for a minute if half of the above population was not allowed to participate in the economy?

It simply means that the impact on the economy would be devastating. Of the population above, 77.7 percent are whites. The remainder are people of color. Why would a nation think she can afford to deprive 22 percent of her citizens of privileges? Are there some benefits for discrimination?

Examples such as the one above will make you think that no able-bodied individual or a group of people should be singled out for denied privileges because it will hurt the economy of a growing nation. If America practiced systemic racism, perhaps there were some advantages for white folks.

Let us see what the benefits of racism are. An article from *Atlanta Blackstar* posted online by A. Moore on September 17, 2014, makes for a very good read. With a few diagrams and few words, the paper lays out eight benefits of racism. Here they are below.

FIG 3

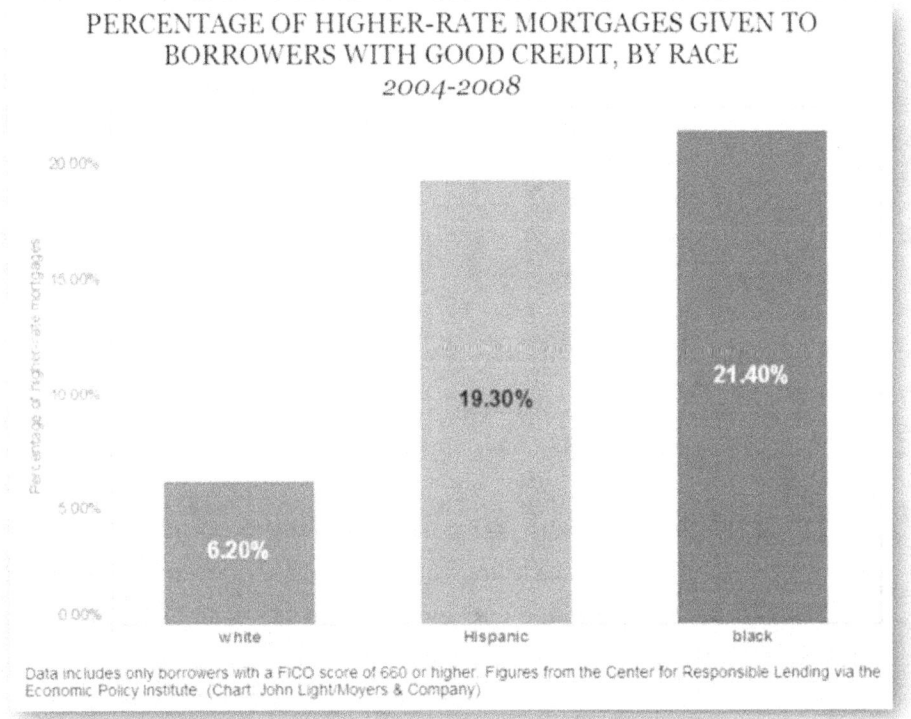

PERCENTAGE OF HIGHER-RATE MORTGAGES GIVEN TO BORROWERS WITH GOOD CREDIT, BY RACE
2004-2008

Data includes only borrowers with a FICO score of 660 or higher. Figures from the Center for Responsible Lending via the Economic Policy Institute (Chart John Light/Moyers & Company)

Whites tend to get better loan rates, a very useful perk if you want to live in those better neighborhoods or start a business.

Even children were discriminated against. If you think for once that such was made up, here, below are the statistics. Please do tell, how can "normal" beings be so cruel as to proscribe racism for kids? Keep your answer to yourself for now. Here is FIG 4

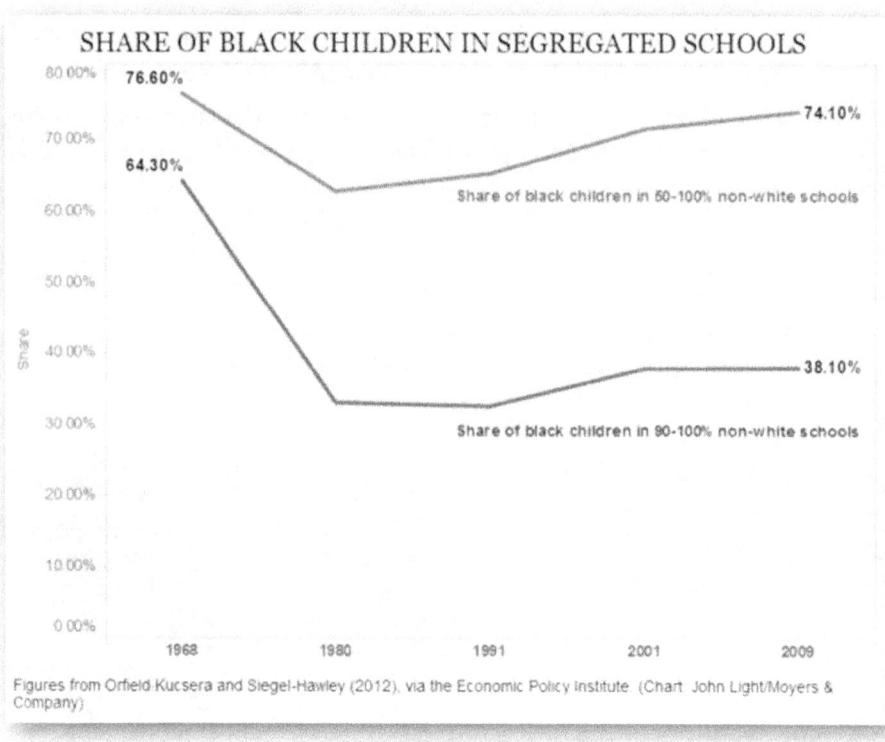

SHARE OF BLACK CHILDREN IN SEGREGATED SCHOOLS

They get to live in nicer, safer neighborhoods with better schools.

Still on capitalism/racism, racism helps promote and makes stronger a concept called capitalism. Blacks are quarantined in neighborhoods like fishes in an artificial lake and harvested to fill up jails, where they are used for free labor whenever the need arises.

Blacks are used to fill the private, newly constructed prisons in order to justify the buildings' existence. And such private prison companies are traded in the New York Stock Exchange. It is like trading slaves in 1704. As much as slave trade seems to have changed, it has remained the same. People are making huge profits out of the imprisonment of black folks.

The company involved—Corrections Corporations of America—is listed on New York Stock Exchange.

Look @ FIG 5

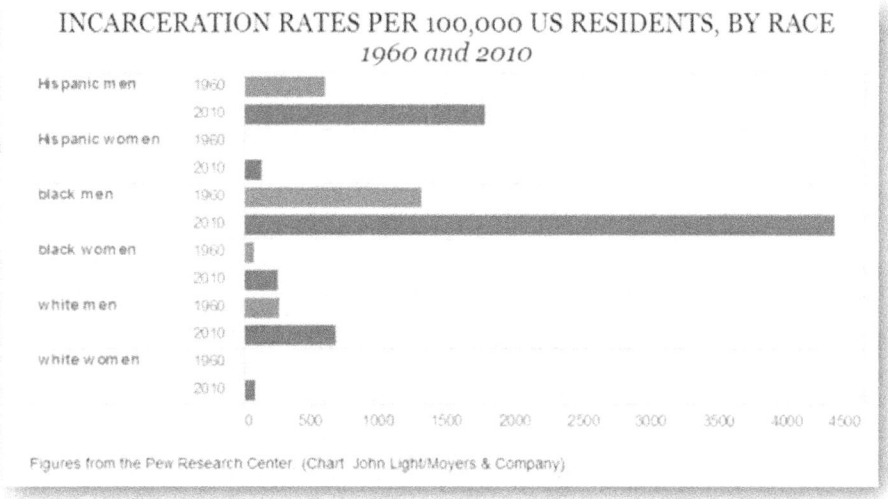

INCARCERATION RATES PER 100,000 US RESIDENTS, BY RACE
1960 and 2010

Figures from the Pew Research Center. (Chart John Light/Moyers & Company)

Whites have lower incarceration rates because their neighborhoods are not targeted for overpolicing. Also, laws are not unfairly written to make sure they do time—and more of it.

Why would the police want to incarcerate any white man or one of the landowners at every turn like they do with nonwhites? It's simple. The police are comprised mostly of white men who police all the neighbohoods—black or white—and most importantly, those neighborhoods where the 1-percenters, otherwise known as the landowners or the corporations, live. There must be that privilege. That unspoken privilege of not being nonwhite. You just cannot mess with the unspoken privilege of the status quo.

Today, one can argue that policing practices and operations are the same worldwide. The exception is that in some countries police have respect for the sanctity of lives—*all* lives. Of course, most societies in the world are not racist societies.

Available statistics point to one fact: police kill more people in racist societies. Though other societies also have their own issues, like class differences, police in such societies do not single out a group for target practice, even if the majority of the police are comprised mostly of white officers.

Another racist society was/is apatheid South Africa. In fact, the state-mandated racial discrimination policies against people of color during the rise of the antiapartheid groups between 1960s and 1980s created racial hostility between the white rulers and people of color. That hostility, combined with incessant violent police actions in the name of the status quo, set ethical liabilities on present-day police operational tactics. Although there have been efforts to improve the socioeconomic burden racism had placed on nonwhites in South Africa, such efforts will not make people of color at par with the rich minority whites, nor will such efforts change police behavior overnight.

In racist societies, policing had adopted those antics borrowed from benchmarks set during slave years. Police tend to see the nonwhite citizens through the same prism they did in the days of legislated discrimination. Old habits are difficult to let go.

CAPITALISM AND THOSE ALLOWED TO PARTICIPATE

This is not the days of slavery, but you can imagine that this diagram will be very different. Even in 2010, below, you can read about the disparity in wealth. In a subsequent chapter, there is a discussion on those who really hold the wealth because not all white people are rich. You may wish to refer to FIG 1 again here.

Below is a women's median weekly earnings by race. FIG 6

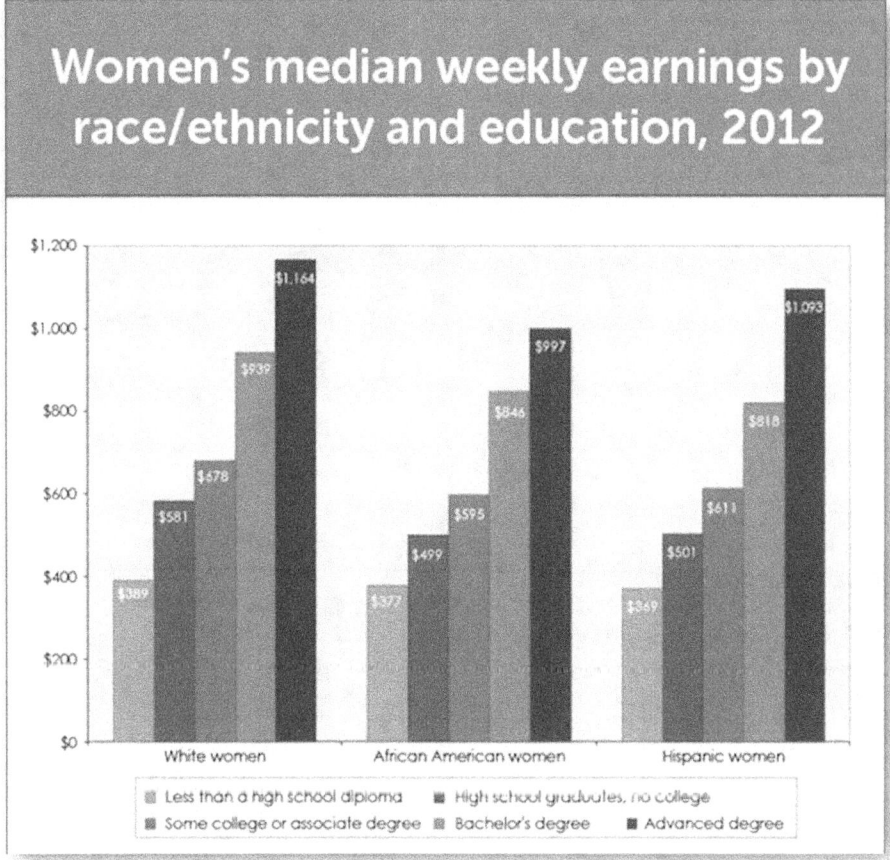

Whites get paid more for the same work and level of qualification.

FIG 7 below

Chart 1: Unemployment Rate for African Americans, Hispanics and Whites
(seasonally adjusted monthly data, January 2007 - January 2012)

African American
Peak Unemployment : 16.7%
August 2011

Hispanic
Peak Unemployment: 13.1%
November 2010

White
Peak Unemployment: 9.3%
October 2009

Source: Bureau of Labor Statistics, Current Population Survey

*Lower unemployment: Whites are less likely to be fired and
more likely to be hired—even with a prison record.*

FIG 8

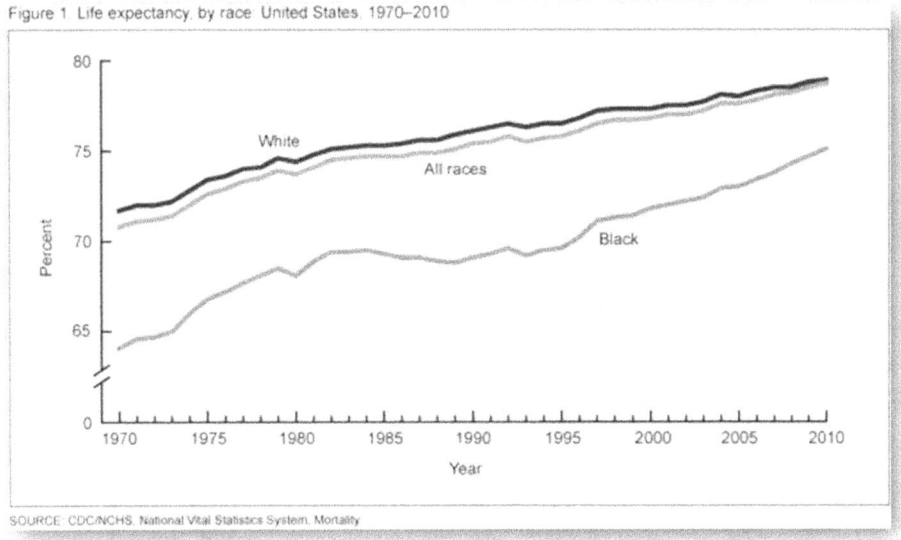

Figure 1. Life expectancy, by race: United States, 1970–2010

Whites live longer: Even poor whites live longer than middle-class blacks.

These are privileges that were assigned to benefit a group, or privileges that were forbidden for people of color.

IS SLAVERY OVER?

The way I observed it . . .

During slavery, the slaves were in chains. They could be marked. They were punished for something, anything—or nothing. The owner had all the say. The slave could be shot. He is the possession of the owner. A property he is. You can appreciate the listed methods for dishing out punishment.

Such absurdity and cruelty you might think ended with the Emancipation Proclamation and the subsequent Thirteenth Amendment. The Thirteenth Amendment formally abolished slavery in the United States. It passed the Senate on April 8, 1864, and the House on January 31, 1865.

On February 1, 1865, President Abraham Lincoln approved the Joint Resolution of Congress submitting the proposed amendment to the state legislatures. The necessary number of states ratified it by December 6, 1865.

The Thirteenth Amendment to the United States Constitution provides that "Neither slavery nor involuntary servitude, except as a punishment for crime whereof the party shall have been duly convicted, shall exist within the United States, or any place subject to their jurisdiction."

Were the slaves really free? If you peruse that document carefully, you will see the caveat in the exception clause of that amendment. It was a trick. A very sinister trick. Can you see the hidden barrier to freedom? It was the setup.

On signed documents, it seems like freedom. The slaves had become freedmen and had the freedoms that all citizens of the United States of America have had. So, we are made to think, accept, and believe.

It takes understanding of the system to start to see the charade freedom has become in the United States of America. The walls that fenced people of color did not crumble with the "freedom." Instead, more walls were built to cage, segregate, discriminate, and, yes, reduce the black race in America.

In parts of America, the Jim Crow laws were introduced, they used semantics such as *separate but equal* to let these wicked laws take hold. Jim Crow laws were statutes and ordinances established between 1874 and 1975 to separate the white and nonwhite races in the American South. In theory, it was to create "separate but equal" treatment, but in practice, Jim Crow laws condemned nonwhites, especially black citizens, to inferior treatment and facilities. And the United States Supreme

Court gave Jim Crow laws credence. The "separate but equal" standard established by the Supreme Court in *Plessy v. Ferguson* (1896) lent high judicial support to segregation.

How can you say a people is free yet go ahead to seek ways to punish and debase them? The question that all Americans must answer is: Are the punishments over yet? If not, why not? Are all Americans treated equally where you live?

In your day-to-day activities, do you see segregation? Do you believe all Americans are treated equally? If you don't see it, it is because it is hidden. There are hidden barriers that keep many people down, and they were designed as a setup for failures.

If you are white, would you love to be treated the way you perceive blacks are treated? If no, why not?

As an aside, other countries in the Americas learned from the United States. Argentina went a little farther. They devised and implemented a means to wipe off the black race from the population. It is no accident that only Argentina is 97 percent white in the Americas.

If you want to learn how the rulers of Argentina implemented their genocide on black people, a little online research will do. The truth of the wickedness of our forefathers is not hidden if you ask the right questions.

The next time the football FIFA World Cup congregates, pay attention to the lineup of Argentina. They are usually the only nation in the Americas with an all-white squad. There is a reason for that.

Ordinarily, some people of color do not even understand how they are all caged in. They buy one franchised Dunkin' Donut, and they think they have arrived. They possess one bodega, and yikes, they think they have become architects of their daily lives. They establish one Shaolin restaurant on the streets of an urban city, and they beat their chest in pride and believe they have made it in the United States.

These people (usually immigrants) must not be denied the sense of accomplishments and well-being they exude. They are entitled to feel that way. Some of them have the luxury of citizenship of two countries.

One, they work under any circumstances for years in any country, and a second country where they return to, is actually where they enjoy true freedom. Some return to their native countries where they will not be subjected to the inhumanity that the black man has endured in their home of the United States for years.

If you critically study the situation in all of the Americas, you begin to wonder how and why the black man survived all the injustices. Perhaps, the black race in America owes the landowners a thank-you (not a demand for an apology) for their survival, for, as we have found, the blacks in Argentina suffered a genocide. A thing that "never" happened in the United States.

Perhaps the African Americans owe the white man a shipload of thanks. After all, the children of slaves survived up to this day. They barely survived the Islamic Arab world and the slave trade that held sway across the Sahara for over 1,400 years—over 14 centuries.

Perhaps black folks should be thankful that slavery in the Americas lasted less than four centuries. They did not survive in Argentina. It was not like Argentina tolerated the slaves after their hard labor was tapped out and slavery was abolished. As the hard labor was tapped out, their lives were systematically snuffed out in that country too.

Now, Argentina has no black population or any problems today . . . or do they?

America took a different route. Incarceration was the route. If you look at state and federal budgets, you will be amazed at what you find. There is a trend. The trend is that both states and the federal government spend more on prisoners than on students. That does not mean that the government prioritizes jails over schools, but that is what the spending trend shows.

You are not about to accept that a racist society like ours is about to love the mostly black prisoners over education, but then, the societies are better off, so it seems, to spend more to lock up prisoners, most of whom are blacks. For those making policy decisions, it is better than spending such money on training or educating potential prisoners, most of whom are nonwhites.

Slavery or incarceration—which is better? That is the point.

CHAPTER 5

The Cato Human
Freedom Index

———

FROM ITS WEB SITE YOU get a detailed description of what it stands for.

> *The Cato Institute is a public policy research organization—a think tank—dedicated to the principles of individual liberty, limited government, free markets, and peace. Its scholars and analysts conduct independent, nonpartisan research on a wide range of policy issues.*
>
> *Founded in 1977, Cato owes its name to Cato's Letters, a series of essays published in 18th-century England that presented a vision of society free from excessive government power. Those essays inspired the architects of the American Revolution. And the simple, timeless principles of that revolution—individual liberty, limited government, and free markets—turn out to be even more powerful in today's world of global markets and unprecedented access to information than Jefferson or Madison could have imagined. Social and economic freedom is not just the best policy for a free people; it is the indispensable framework for the future.*

How Cato is funded . . .

In order to maintain its independence, the Cato Institute accepts no government funding. Cato receives approximately 80 percent of its funding through tax-deductible contributions from individuals, with the remainder of its support coming from foundations, corporations, and the sale of books and publications.

It is refreshing that there are organizations such as the Cato Institute. Such institutes filter all the noise and feed you factual realities.

Really? Let's accept it is so. However, do not discount that corporations contribute to it financially.

Like me, you may have guessed that the United States will top the list and stayed at the top. After all, the United States is the proclaimed "land of the free." No other nations will even come a distant second. The land where, among other phrases, you have "Give me freedom or give me death."

If you are used to the propaganda disseminated by the powerful few media house, you would not be faulted for accepting that our freedoms are intact and guaranteed.

But who is behind the information we have come to accept as the truth? Who owns the channels of all communications? The few rich men—the 1-percenters own them all.

Forget the angry faces and voices of some of the people being the talking heads. They are nothing but the voice of the masters. They are the middle class doing the masters' bidding. They are middle class thanks to the landowners.

These talking heads will be silenced if the master so says. You may even believe that the most threats to our freedoms come from foreigners. The truth of the matter is that foreigners have little or nothing to do with our freedoms.

Our freedoms have been set from the beginning by the capitalists, otherwise known as the rich big landowners—the slave masters. As time passed, the calibration of the freedoms has been left to governments—local, state, and federal.

Though the Supreme Court reflected the opinions of those ugly years, though the armed forces succumbed to the practices of segregation and outright discrimination, both departments were quick to rise to the good side of our freedoms.

This does not exclude the armed forces from doing the masters' bidding.

When it comes to determining freedoms, Cato Institute has a fine criteria of evaluating countries. Cato publishes its annual *Human Freedom Index*, ranking over 150 countries in the world according to their level of liberty enjoyed by their citizens.

The U.S. occupies the twentieth spot, down from its seventeenth spot in 2014, thus reflecting the deteriorating freedoms and also a drop in adherence to the rule of law. It might be surprising to some but absolutely not surprising to Americans of color.

Some other criteria used in the rankings—the index Cato published here presents a broad measure of human freedoms, understood as the absence of coercive constraint. Cato usually uses 76 distinct indicators of personal and economic freedom in the following areas of:

Rule of Law
Security and Safety
Movement
Religion
Association, Assembly, and Civil Society
Expression
Relationships
Size of Government
Legal System and Property Rights
Access to Sound Money
Freedom to Trade Internationally
Regulation of Credit, Labor, and Business

Of the various indicators used—rule of law and regulation of credit, labor, and business stand out.

Some will opine that the U.S. rank has declined since the year 2000 as the war on terror, the war on drugs, and a weakening of property rights have taken their toll on liberty in America. The truth is that from the beginning, though the rule of law has existed as a concept, it did not apply to all Americans the same way. The rule of law meant different things to rich white men, it means another to the middle class, and it means something much more different to colored America.

To those who understood and have complained about America's type of freedoms, the placement of the United States scores of seventeenth and twentieth in the Cato human freedom index were no surprise. It will never be a surprise either in the near future.

It cannot be any worse that Africa's Mauritius beat America to it too. To many nonwhites, none of these scores tell a new story. They are just an affirmation of what they already knew. Remember that America was, at one point in time, worse than apartheid South Africa.

Part of the Cato article reads:

Hong Kong and Switzerland top the rankings, followed in order by Finland, Denmark, New Zealand, and Canada. The United States ranks in 20th place, below the United Kingdom (9) and Chile (18). Other countries rank as follows: Singapore (43), India (75), Russia (111), China (132), Venezuela (144), and Zimbabwe (149).

The United States fell from 17th place in 2008 to 20th place in 2012. The decline reflects a long-term drop in every category of economic freedom and in its rule of law indicators. The U.S. performance is worrisome and shows that the United States can no longer claim to be the leading bastion of liberty in the world. In addition to the expansion of the regulatory state and drop in economic freedom, the war on terror, the war on drugs, and the erosion of property rights due to greater use of eminent domain all likely have contributed to the U.S. decline.

We do not measure democracy in the index, though we consider it important. Indeed, we find a strong relationship between human freedom and democracy, a link that merits further study. As such, Hong Kong is an outlier in our index. Its high ranking is due to its traditionally strong rule of law, and high levels of both personal and economic freedom, something that all advocates of freedom, including democracy advocates, should seek to protect. The danger there is that China's efforts to limit democracy will lead to increasing interference in the territory's institutions—including on the independence of its legal system and the freedom of its press—which will reduce its overall freedom.

Frankly, that the United States is not #1 is indicative of a truth. Any nation that would practice two kinds of rule of law must not be rewarded for its apartheid; they must be called out for what they practice—white supremacy.

CHAPTER 6

Destroying the Poor Families

———

SOME ACCUSE HER OF WHORING. They say she has baby daddies. And that she does not know her babies' daddies. You watch *The Maury Povich Show* in the mornings and you observe mostly the poor populace cutting a check out of their miseries on the TV show.

They seek to hear Maury say, "You are the father!" but most often what you hear is, "You are not the father!" They have become objects for TV entertainment for all.

There usually is no man in the household to bring about discipline on the kids. The mama becomes the father. The mother just has to be strong for the family. She's all the black family's got now. Is she really a whore because she has five baby fathers for four kids? If you are in the black woman's situation, you probably would do worse.

According to available information—for every 100 black females not in jail, there are only 44 men—it has gotten that bad. In other words, even if the 44 men were to take two women each, there will still be black women without a man in the households. Thus, 44 men equate to approximately 44 percent of households with a male figure.

When it comes to marriages, a Yale University study found that just 42 percent of black women are married. But researchers Ivory A.

Toldson of Howard University and Bryant Marks of Morehouse College question the accuracy of this finding.

Employing census data from 2005 to 2009, Toldson and Marks found that 75 percent of black women marry before they turn age 35.

Whether they stayed married depends on many variables.

In an article in the *New York Times*, "The Methodology: 1.5 Million Missing Black Men," the authors screamed, "For every 100 black women not in jail, there are only 83 black men. The remaining men—1.5 million of them—are, in a sense, missing."

Please bear in mind that in some black communities, the ratio of men to 100 black women not in jail is much lower than 100:83

Using data collated from the 2010 Census, the trio—Justin Wolfers, David Leonhardt, and Kevin Quealy, writing for *The Upshot* in the *New York Times*, attempted to account for those African American males "missing" from day-to-day life in the U.S.A.

But, who are these missing black males? They are your fathers, grandfathers, sons, cousins, coworkers, students, friends, grandsons, brothers, neighbors, and others. They have human faces, hands, legs, and names.

What struck me most was when the authors wrote, "More than one out of every six black men who today should be between 25 and 54 years old, have disappeared from daily life . . . Remarkably, black women who are 25 to 54 and not in jail outnumber black men in that category by 1.5 million."

Notwithstanding whichever statistics above is nearer the truth, the truth of the matter is that they all acknowledge the systemic incarceration of black people, especially men.

It is worth recollecting a part of the article that acknowledged "Our definition of black is based on individuals describing that as their only race, but an analysis of people who identify themselves as both black and as another race shows the same patterns. An analysis of data from

2013—based on the American Community Survey, which is more recent but less comprehensive than a decennial census—also shows similar conclusions."

This is how much and how bad the policies of those in positions of public authority have devastated the black family.

I can assure you that if the situation was occurring among the white populace on the same scale as nonwhites, there would have been an uproar to correct the policies that brought about those results.

Where there is a man in the family, the man (father) has been so demonized and destroyed that he is likely to have done some jail time. As a nonwhite, his chance of landing a job is most definitely zero. His chance of participating in public programs that will provide shelter and put food on the table has been taken away.

He has been prepped to return to jail even if he did not commit any nonviolent offence. No jobs, no shelter, no food. He cannot even be a man anymore. No dignity.

And the black woman has been forced to be the man for so long, she does not know any more if she needs a man in the home. The black family has been distanced. It was systemic.

And wait—you will soon hear about him stealing a loaf of bread—from the local grocery store. You will hear it from the same landowners' TV outlets, and you blame the armed or unarmed robber.

The media house is very good at informing and reminding you that the grocery store robber is a black male too. They hardly forget that little detail. To them, that is the most important detail. Just so that they can beam the black face of the robber to millions of white homes. Therein lies the biggest achievement and satisfaction.

Where the common thief is shot for stealing a gallon of milk, they say, they feared for their lives. The robber has been demonized and set up to be destroyed. There was a cover for shooting without aiming. The black folks had been demonized.

That was one of the goals.

Or, you hear that he was dealing some $5 reefer (weed) on the corner street knowing fully well that it could be his last day on earth because there is the possibility that he could be shot by either fellow dealers and/or the police, and you wonder why he is hopeless and chose to sacrifice himself on the streets.

There are other avenues to get him. He is supposed to provide free labor while in jail. The black man has been prepped to be missing in action for the family.

That is one of the hidden barriers in the setup.

I think that the black family was intended from the get-go to be destroyed. If you think that that is far-fetched, remember that the destruction of black families was achieved in Argentina. There were no ifs, ands, or buts. From the beginning just prior to setting the slaves "free," the black man was marked and caged. It was even done legally. It was hidden. It was a setup. It was systemically specified in the Thirteenth Amendment.

Let us reason: Why was a provision that was a path to free labor inserted in the Thirteenth Amendment? While it seemed intended to abolish private ownership of slaves, it reintroduced public ownership of slaves by the government through the back door.

Indirectly, the governments—local, state, or federal—can get free labor by convicting a few whites and the majority of nonwhites for free labor. Perhaps the conviction of a handful of poor whites would make it equal and fair.

The Thirteenth Amendment to the United States Constitution provides that "Neither slavery nor involuntary servitude, except as a punishment for crime whereof the party shall have been duly convicted, shall exist within the United States, or any place subject to their jurisdiction."

Did you read the trickery in that whole sentence? It is like muting a TV while having the caption option on. It's a win-win for the landowners. Do you see how the landowners made provisions to cage the black man in America? Do you see the continuation of slavery through the back door? Now, perhaps, you see the reason why the United States incarcerates more prisoners than any nation on earth.

Advocates, too, have noted that the Constitution's Thirteenth Amendment, ratified in 1865, abolished slavery in the United States, but provided that exception in cases where persons have been "duly convicted" in the United States and its territories, slavery or involuntary servitude can be reimposed as a punishment. Thus, it was slavery in your father's days and incarceration in yours. What's the difference?

Who writes the laws for the circumstances under which you are "duly convicted" so that you return to slavery or involuntary servitude?

Perhaps the governments can defend the free labor they get by claiming that the convicts are paid a pittance of wages while incarcerated.

Meanwhile, the economies of the prisons are traded on Wall Street. The trade boomed in the years of Presidents Reagan and Clinton.

The trade continues today on Wall St.

Today, more blacks have gone through the gates to become slaves in prisons than their fathers did from the gates on the coasts of Africa on their way to the Americas.

Today, there are more black men in prisons and on probation than there were slaves in 1850 just before the Civil War.

Do you see the effects of that exception in the Thirteenth Amendment? That clause simply gave power to make laws that will trap those who had already been set up by the system so that any attempt to escape it is impossible.

They make the laws, they interpret the laws, and they execute the laws.

CHAPTER 7

The University of Incarceration: The Prisons

THERE WAS A TIME WHEN people believed that the prisons were accepting more black men than the universities. Needless to say, this garnered much attention in the media, and more than 10 years later, it still serves as a good talking point for encapsulating the social challenges facing nonwhites, especially black men. Below is FIG 9

At one point in time that was also true. Examine the information below:

	Total Black Men in Prison/Jail*	Black Men Enrolled in Postsecondary Education
2000	829,200	717,491
2001	842,000	712,724
2002	851,600	964,056
2003	857,300	1,003,742
2004	826,700	1,014,474
2005	837,700	1,070,591
2006	831,100	1,081,647
2007	858,600	1,107,892
2008	870,800	1,072,536
2009	864,100	1,175,319
2010	844,600	1,341,354

*Source: BJS, National Prisoner Statistics Program, Federal Justice Statistics Program, National Corrections Reporting Program, Survey of Inmates in State and Local Correctional Facilities, and National Inmate Survey 2010.
*Source: Department of Education, National Center for Education Statistics, Integrated Postsecondary Education System, Enrollment Survey 2000-10.

Meanwhile, as people are used to spending most of their prime years in prisons, they have come to accept it as the university for indentured servitude. Thus, it is journey to the university of incarceration that many black men in the United States were prepped for from birth.

They therefore wear it like a badge of honor—a passage of rites, so to speak. They discuss their experiences. They discuss how many times they have been there. First times are toughest, and subsequent times are tough, but at least after the first time you know what to expect. If you are 18–34 years old, the bulls-eye is on your back.

The chances that a black man age 18–34 would attend a regular university is lower than his chances of going to jail.

That is how it was set up. You ask why I say set up. Examine the statistics of all benchmarks that lead to quality of life and you will observe by the facts and figures that the system was set up that way. The hurdles are stacked against black people in the United States.

Studies show that the prison population grew by more than 700 percent from 1970 to 2005, a rate that is outpacing crime and population rates. What is astonishing and dumbfounding is this increase does not include the general population as is. These incarceration rates are impacted by men of color.

Statistics have it that one in every 15 black men in America and one in every 36 Hispanic men are incarcerated. Compare this to one in every 106 white men. The trend is getting worse for people of color over the years.

Today, the statistics indicate that one in every six black men in America is likely to be arrested. One in three black men end up in prison compared to white men. Whatever the statistics, the results are the same: Blacks are far more likely to be arrested than any other racial group in the USA. In some places like Ferguson, Missouri, it is dramatically so.

From the *New York Times* article, April 20, 2015:

"1.5 Million Missing Black Men," by Justin Wolfers, David Leonhardt, and Kevin Quealy summarizes it well here.

In New York, almost 120,000 black men between the ages of 25 and 54 are missing from everyday life. In Chicago, 45,000 are, and more than 30,000 are missing in Philadelphia. Across the South—from North Charleston, S.C., through Georgia, Alabama, and Mississippi and up into Ferguson, Mo.—hundreds of thousands more are missing. They are missing, largely because of early deaths or because they are behind bars. Remarkably, black women who are 25 to 54 and not in jail outnumber black men in that category by 1.5 million, according to an Upshot analysis. For every 100 black women in this age group living outside of jail, there are only 83 black men. Among whites, the equivalent number is 99, nearly parity. African American men have long been more likely to be locked up and more likely to die young, but the scale of the combined toll is nonetheless jarring. It is a measure of the deep disparities that continue to afflict black men—disparities being debated after a recent spate of killings by the police—and the gender gap is itself a further cause of social ills, leaving many communities without enough men to be fathers and husbands.

This gap, driven mostly by incarceration and early deaths barely exists among the white folks. Within the white community it is one missing white man for every 100 white women. You can see the disparity further when you compare the population of blacks to whites.

According to the National Association for the Advancement of Colored People (NAACP), African Americans constitute nearly 1 million of the total 2.3 million incarcerated populations, and have nearly six times the rate of whites.

It would be nice to remind the reader again that the proportion of blacks in the total population of the United States is between 12 to 13 percent. The situation is now so dire that for every three black men born today, one is guaranteed a "luxurious" room—in jail. This is scary.

An African American male born in the 1990s has approximately 30 percent chance of spending time in prison at some point in his life.

Black males ages 30 to 34 have the highest incarceration rate in the United States and the world.

Now, have you started to ask of yourself "How come so many blacks are jail bound?" Have you just figured that most of those who are lucky to make it to that age range perhaps struggled through life without a father because the father has been hauled away to jail for "good" reasons . . . or no reason whatsoever?

It is the system. It is systemic.

If other races, like white, are systematically decimated in this fashion, changes would have been made a long time ago. The outcry would have been so thunderously white that changes to the system would have been effected immediately.

At this rate, one wonders how the black race has continued to thrive.

Statistics has it that one out of nine African American men will be incarcerated between the ages of 20 and 34. The key to decimating any family is to yank the head of the household—the man. For the black family, the head had been yanked a very long time ago. When there is no head, there is no direction. It was intentionally planned that way. It's the system.

The black population is under a simulated-controlled experiment. Did I use the word . . . *experiment*?

Sorry!

The truth of the matter is that most people are becoming conscious, or like some would say—becoming *better educated*. They are beginning to be conscious of the dirty tricks.

The plan is working perfectly well . . . as intended. It was a plan for social, economic, and political control. It has been so historically, *and* in contemporary American society. It sounds monotonous when you read that blacks make up 12 percent of the population yet provide approximately 50 percent of all the incarcerated in America.

Have you thought about why this is so? If you are white and have never thought about this, give it some thought. Would *you* like to be treated like the black folks have been?

Let us look for a clue.

It was not by accident that the black family was targeted for decimation. It was a well thought out plan. When you observe the how, you see that it is all concocted. You need not be too smart to see how all the variables fall into place.

Even apartheid South Africa was not as neck deep in a simulated and controlled experiment—oh, sorry—*plan*! Even at her white peak, apartheid South Africa did not come up with a Thirteenth Amendment kind of exception to incarcerate as many of the black men like the United States did.

I remember an interview by Ted Koppel on ABC's *Nightline*. He was interviewing a South African minister. He was also subtly castigating the minister about apartheid practices. After some tough questions, the minister snapped and made some indicting statements to the effect "You are no better," meaning America has no moral ground to stand to chastise South Africa. Ted Koppel had no reply.

The issue is not only the arrests per se, though the arrests are an issue. The issues are too varied as much as they are planned and implemented to decimate an ethnic group. One of those issues is the application of privileges and the implementation of the rule of law.

Most of us erroneously believe that the rule of law is applied equitably. If you believe that, perhaps, you are nonblack.

The rule of law requires the government to exercise its power in accordance with well-established and clearly written rules, regulations, and legal principles. A distinction is sometimes drawn between power, will, and force, on the one hand, and law, on the other.

When a government official acts pursuant to an express provision of a written law, he acts within the rule of law. But when a government official acts without the imprimatur of any law, he or she does so by the sheer force of personal will and power.

The exception in the Thirteenth Amendment seems to have been written for the sheer force of government will and power.

The rule of law does not mean one interpretation and shorter sentences for some people and a different interpretation and tougher and longer sentences for others. But that is exactly what has occurred over time. It is unspoken, but people understand.

The amendment (exception) to the Thirteenth Amendment was a path to undue punishment. Whether you liken it to indentured servitude or slavery, you are within the confines of the truth.

Have you ever wondered what the rule of law means? This was translation culled from legal-dictionary.thefreedictionary.com/Ruleoflaw.

> *The rule of law is an ambiguous term that can mean different things in different contexts. In one context, the term means rule according to law. No individual can be ordered by the government to pay civil damages or suffer criminal punishment except in strict accordance with well-established and clearly defined laws and procedures. In a second context, the term means rule under law. No branch of government is above the law, and no public official may act arbitrarily or unilaterally outside of the law. In a third context, the term means rule according to a higher law. No written law may be enforced by the government unless it conforms with certain unwritten, universal principles of fairness, morality, and justice that transcend the human legal system.*

That there are so many black people incarcerated does not mean that there are no black lawyers, doctors, nurses, surgeons, police, presidents, etc. They are the exceptions—not the norm. They too face predatory policing. They too live in neighborhoods where predatory policing applies.

Predatory policing is a practice set up to generate arrests even in the face of a rule of law. The ongoing struggle for freedoms and justice continues. For some Americans, it must continue. It is a good investment when we invest our civic capital in the undertaking to achieve the ideal balance between liberty and order, law and reason, while trying to reconcile freedom and security. What happens though, when atrocities are preprogrammed to occur through systemic legislation by those in positions of authority without consideration to the rule of law when it concerns people of color is highly troubling.

What should baffle anyone to a huge extent is that the same people who are suffering under the exception contained in the Thirteenth Amendment are the same population that partly empower the political class.

CHAPTER 8

Your Zip Code, Your Food Type

———

YOUR ZIP CODE DECIDES THE quality of food you get to buy. Most often, your zip code decides how much you pay for your food. In some neighborhoods, it is very expensive to be poor.

In stores located near or in neighborhoods of color, you are more likely to get products that are costly and unhealthy. You get products that should have been marked "Eat and be obese." Others could be marked as "Drink me and slowly become diabetic."

You hardly can get stores carrying fruits, let alone organic ones. Most convenience stores carry a wide variety of chips, colorful candies, bottles, and plastics of sugary carbonated beverages. Almost all shoppers buy these available calorie-loaded foods wrapped in beautiful packages.

What is wrong here?

What is wrong is that shoppers cannot find fresh produce, whole grains, and low-fat dairy products necessary for a healthy diet. These stores, as you can tell, are the only nearby food source for millions of Americans living in such neighborhoods. In these stores, if you find fruits, they are usually packaged in cans. These convenient stores are simply isolated from affordable, healthy food.

Meanwhile, you have liquor stores on every other block. You have a fried chicken restaurant on every other block. You cannot find a bookstore. It is as if everything was strategically planned to assist in suffocating the people.

It is just so.

Mayor Michael Bloomberg of New York City recognized the issues with neighborhood foods. He understood the medical cost to the city of New York. He stopped smoking in restaurants. He also tried to push it a little. He wanted to limit the size of sugary drinks in public places.

The courts were not friendly to the soda limit idea. The courts think that people can make better choices.

Do they?

The courts should have stood by two streets to observe the people. They should have stood on Adam Clayton Powell by Seventh Avenue and 125th Street in New York City. They should just observe the passersby. They could count all the skinny persons on one hand. Even most of the teenagers are obese.

One hour on a hot sunny day will do. On a hot day, most people will have parts of their bodies exposed. By the way, it is worth mentioning that organic vegetables and fruits were displayed and sold right in front of the Adam Clayton Powell Building.

Many workers around this area spend their breaks having lunch on those organic fruits for the duration of time I was in the vicinity. The fruits were not necessarily more expensive.

If the court had also stood and observed the people on Times Square by Forty-second, the difference is very striking. It is the opposite of the earlier observation.

In fact, the New York City Department of Health launched a program with the aim of reaching the teens 13 to 19 in various neighborhoods of the Bronx, Brooklyn, and Manhattan. The aim is to reach and teach the teens about health and food. Recent city data found that approximately 12 percent of students under 18 years were obese.

They were mostly black and Latino kids. Food companies tend to increase their advertisements for products like gum, snacks, candy, and sugary drinks, especially in minority communities.

It is a no-brainer that eating habits affect our health and longevity. What is available in your corner store? You may need a ride to some far distant locations to get quality, healthy, and cheap foods. Various studies by food and nutrition researchers exposed the disparity or unequal distribution of food stores in various communities of the rich, middle class, and the poor class.

One study covered access to stores for people using food stamps. Food stamps are government checks given periodically to people who are in need. The other study looked at shopping in areas far removed from some heavily populated neighborhoods of big cities. Healthy foods available at supermarkets, grocery, and convenience stores far removed from big cities were looked into.

The two studies found access to healthy food is most problematic in low-income neighborhoods. Of course, these neighborhoods are predominantly black or Latino. Eating right is like a checking and savings account. You can choose to save or incur expenses. It is your account.

You spend what you have. So far, nonwhites and poor people tend to suffer and die earlier than rich and middle-class people. Obviously, the more nature in your food, the better for your health.

What is in *your* food?

CHAPTER 9

Slavery or Incarceration?

STATISTICS HAVE IT THAT AT this moment there are more black men locked up or in some federal or state penitentiary. More are under parole supervision than there were slaves in the 1850s. In the 1850s, you may as well have said blacks were incarcerated as slaves in the masters' compounds and you would not be wrong.

Today, the black man is "free." Yet, he is incarcerated in larger numbers than ever. If you really think about it, the black man was freer when he was a slave because less black men were in jails. They were busy at work.

It was as if there were no choices. For all of history in the United States, the black man was either the master's slave or the government's slave through "trick" incarceration. Neither one is good, but both accomplish the goal of keeping the black man down and out.

The black man's plight is irredeemable as long as the setup of those hidden barriers—those roadblocks we refer to as systemic—remain. But the black man—*all* black men in America—need not only understand this plight, they must act politically through the ballots to demand changes.

Marching alone cannot and has not been able to do it. So far, voting democratic all the time does not seem to shift the posts in the laws that keep the black race down in the United States.

Attending colleges and achieving many degrees which require you to start begging for jobs would not wholly cut it. Perhaps you know a middle-class family without a college degree.

The point is, if after graduating college and you have a résumé in hand begging for a job, you may have to reevaluate your line of study. Sometimes learning crafts will provide you a job, a quality of life and economic freedoms far better than what you have been forced to study for many years.

Who fixes your car? Who does your plumbing? Who built your house . . . or better yet, who did you buy your house from? All these crafts are available in community colleges. If everybody becomes a lawyer, I would like to control what they eat for breakfast, lunch, and sometimes, dinner. I wouldn't mind being a restauranteur and make a franchise out of it.

Whether a black man—*any* black man—made a million dollars, that would not shield him from the same suspicions that the average black man endures while shopping in a brick-and-mortar store. While many may think that the black man's plight in the 1850s was much worse, a critical review of the black men's lives today shows a situation no better than it was during slavery.

A day in a black man's life compared to a white man's day might illustrate it better.

Have you ever in a day of your life felt like a marked man? It must be a terrible feeling. Have you ever been to a place where you know all eyes are on you, not because you are a celebrity, but because you are marked as an individual who is about to steal or behave badly?

And all the eyes don't even understand that *they* are the reason you are the way you are. They denied you all that makes life worthwhile while they enjoy privileges that are out of your reach.

You have been marked by the society. The society has low expectations of you. Unfortunately, it is that same society that has put all the hidden barriers in the setup to ensure that your expectations are never fulfilled. Sounds wicked? If it does, that is because it . . . is wicked.

How can people just hate you intrinsically for your being?

Do you drive while black and scared? Have you seen police officers while driving, and you panic? Not all police officers are good cops. And not all cops are bad.

In America there is the KKK—a group of people who believe that they are gods on earth. You must look like them or else you are no good. They have done many bad things. They live in the society. They make up the society. Part of the society is the police, the Congress, the governments, and all facets of the society. They are in the police, in governments, in business, etc.

Can you perceive why when a black man is arrested for just a few milligrams of weed, then sometimes they turn up dead a few hours later? Or you wonder why a young black man—sometimes a child—gets shot before the officer asks questions.

Enslaved. Incarcerated. Shot. What is the difference? Where is the freedom?

The black populace has always been the trump card in the games that the rich capitalists engage in. It was the reason for the Civil War. The war was not about the freedoms of the slaves. It was a war about how to share the labors of the black man in the emerging capitalism.

And they came to an agreement with the creation of the Thirteenth Amendment. The exception in that amendment would lead various regions in the United States and its territories to come up with laws to fish for black men.

Always remember this: The first slaves were not black. They were convicted death-row European whites sold to rich white landowners in the New World. Also remember that their numbers were not enough to do the enormous work in the fields. Enough numbers or not, the white slaves found it hard to adapt to the elements of the environments in which they found themselves. The white skin hardly can spend that many hours in the sun.

Hence, the need for more hands. They borrowed the idea of black slavery from the Arabs. The Arabs had been in this trade for over 14 centuries. Approximately 30 million black slaves died in the hands of the Arabs. With the Arab slave traders, the ratio of slaves purchased or as bounties of war were 3:2 ratio of women: men. The men were mostly castrated, and the women were kept in harems to fulfill sexual needs. Most often if those women became pregnant, the resulting baby's head was smashed on stones if they were male.

Enter the rich white male landowner. He acquired black slaves in the ratio 4 males:1 female. His intention was to work the farms. He allowed the slaves to have families. The males were not neutered. They figured, why castrate the males when they can be used to increase the slave population.

Slaves were killed as punishments—all slaves—white or black. They were killed to serve as witness to others who would have any ambitious thoughts to do what the executed slaves dared to do.

Then suddenly, the execution of white slaves stopped.

It was a privilege. It was the beginning of white privilege. It was the beginning of the game. The game of *we against them*. The white poor slaves thought *Perhaps we are better off than the black slaves since the rich white men won't kill us anymore.*

Soon, more privileges were added to the white slaves.

White slaves could buy back themselves and thus, pursue economic well-being. They could be freemen.

It was and still is—a game. And the rich white capitalists would go far to perfect it. Today, there are many white people who believe that they were freemen because they are white, but they don't know that they were freed so as to serve as a wall of defense for the rich landowners—the

1 percent. Not all white people are rich. And they definitely were not rich then.

Like all societies, there were the bad, the good, and the ugly. There were the poor and the rich. All humans have a desire for food, shelter, and security. The desire for security was the #1 priority of the rich and famous.

With the uprising in Haiti, the priority for security went astronomically high. The rich landowners understood the situation. They had a hand to play, and they played it well.

They played the hand called "divide and conquer" or the "we against them" or the "us and them." Today, it is simply known as the "race card."

America's poor white slaves were then undoubtedly made to get richer in aggregate, and the percentage of people in the United States living in extreme poverty was therefore made lower than ever before. And the poor white slaves thought they belonged.

The superrich cleverly buffered themselves against any slave insurrection.

The rich big landowners in the United States and across the Atlantic watched, learned, and took notice. You can now understand why the game of *we against them* worked then and is still working perfectly today.

Now, it is reasonable and understandable to see why America was the way it was then and the way it is now. Even the architects of the American way then were big landowners and rich white men. They were protecting their greedy interests.

That interest was and still is . . . Capitalism.

CHAPTER 10

The Slaves of Capitalism

———

THE WAY I INTERPRETED IT . . .

Do you want to hazard a guess why the United States is the #1 incarceration nation?

Let's look for some clues.

The first is because the mostly incarcerated people are black people. If they were whites, incarceration would be limited to only heinous crimes.

Remember the Thirteenth Amendment and the exception contained therein? The new nation must provide a means to feed the emerging capitalism with labor. It's slavery by imprisonment.

There are two ways to accomplish this.

Firstly, through involuntary servitude or involuntary slavery. It is a legal and constitutional term for any person laboring against their will while benefitting another, under some form of coercion.

Today, most people still do serious labor except that they get paid. Your pay is often not negotiated as it would have been predetermined unless you work for self.

If you work for corporations, do not kid yourself; you are under involuntary servitude with pay. The pay is one of the differences. You also sign up for the job.

Secondly, even though slavery was abolished, a means to acquire free labor was provided for. This time, it is through incarceration of the children of slaves to provide free labor. It was not a complicated plan. The planners were in the position and with power to craft, interpret, and enforce laws. They can simply craft a law that prohibits and makes marijuana a forbidden plant. The point here is not the plant; it is simply a means to capture and fill up the jails for free labor.

You can't help but reflect and appreciate how vital Indian hemp was to the success of this country. Some of the goods that are made from Indian hemp are paper, rope, clothing fabric, and others. Somehow, along our journey, Indian hemp suddenly found its way up to the schedule 1 drug list.

"Make the most you can of the Indian hemp seed and sow it everywhere."

"Hemp is of first necessity to the wealth & protection of the country."

"Some of my finest hours have been spent sitting on my back veranda, smoking hemp, and observing as far as my eye can see."

All three of these quotes were attributed to our Founding Fathers. Not only that, Thomas Jefferson also drafted the Declaration of Independence on hemp paper as well. OK, back to capitalism.

The Thirteenth Amendment was a well thought out plan. They knew what they were doing. They planned it superbly. It was a simple plan—tell the world that we abolished slavery while scooping free labor by arresting and incarcerating the same citizens.

Capitalism, of course, was one of the reasons for mass incarcerations.

The black prisoner-slaves of capitalism you might say were and are ignorant. That, perhaps, is the truth. They were prepped to be ignorant in a white man's "land." It is always easy to lead the blind, so it is no surprise that some people were meant to be miseducated or not educated at all.

Can you name one more reason for the input of an exception to the Thirteenth Amendment? Think about it and decide.

Should you say, slaves of capitalism or prisoners of capitalism, or, by another slick description—involuntary servitude? Involuntary servitude best describes the American music industry. Perhaps you will agree that Michael Jackson's, James Brown's, and Prince's level of musical genius were almost scary. The landowner's engagement in slavery was evil yet genius in the use of slaves as much as it was also certainly scary. You can be doing involuntary servitude and not know it.

Capitalism is the reason America is the way America is. Capitalism is the reason for racism. Capitalism means that a few people must be at the top while a handful are made to feel like they belong because they are classified as middle class (the resulting upgrade from poor white slaves).

Capitalism, then, means, that a great number of others must be kept down. The groups that must be kept down also include whites, blacks, and the other 99 variables of black.

To make capitalism work, the following structures must be in place to put all the groups of middle class and poor peoples in their place.

By the way, middle class is as much a matter of perception as it is statistics. It also depends on how you define middle class and/or who you take your definition from. For some, middle class is the quality of life and how you go about achieving it. Some want to quantify it in the amount of money they have accumulated. In some places, a middle-class man in America can be an economic god in another country.

Just like slaves were very important for the success of capitalism, there must be other organizations to make this American-type capital-ism succeed. The type that allows landowners full participation while making other white folks believe that they are participating by providing security for the landowners. Black folks, while being the workhorses, were prohibited from participating.

Some of these departments have varied functions, but the composition of their members tell a good story. Let us look at three of the organizations. They are police, the courts, and the prisons.

CHAPTER 11

The Police & the Courts

To SOME OF US, THE police are to serve the general public. Their job is to maintain peace and arrest those few people who would make living unbearable for the law-abiding citizenry.

In most communities, that is what the police are supposed to do. What police do in capitalist and racist societies, like apartheid South Africa and the United States, includes that . . . and much more.

It is assumed and usually said that the people (taxpayers) pay the police. That is another way of implying that the police must listen to the people. While that is true, the truth of the matter is that focus is taken from where focus is needed.

Who controls the police?

The answer to this question would shine some light on whom the police are responsible to. If you theorize that the police are responsible to you, obviously, you are one of the rich, big landowners or one of the 10 percent that own 90 percent of the resources or the middle-class white populace whose thinking is shaped by the rich landowners.

For black men in the United States, the police have always been the slave catchers, whether slaves yesterday or prisoners today.

No matter how you look at it, the police were the creation of capitalists/oligarchs to keep poor people in check. Common sense would have made it clear to most people and especially mayors in today's large cities of America, that poor communities are wont to have strife, insurrections, hunger, etc.

Some mayors have argued that poor communities need the police and more policing than other communities because criminal activities in poor neighborhoods are very high. What they will not tell you is that the planners of what we must hear, eat, and drink were also the same planners of where poor people must live and how they live.

They were the same people who would introduce drugs in poor neighborhoods and let the people fight and kill one another, while they turn around to arrest murderers and drug dealers to fill the prisons. Never ever forget that some people are making money and getting rich off of ruined nonwhite lives.

If society must keep poor people in check, then why not use the people from the poor communities to police their communities? Perhaps it's been figured out that, that would definitely reduce poverty, but the ability to control the nonwhite population may have been lost. Another important loss would be the ability to fill the prisons with black people. And so, the capitalism—sorry—systemic racism—continues.

The Police Departments

You need no one to tell you that police departments all across America are comprised mostly of white officers. It was and still is deliberate. It has always been deliberate. But with the push by the Justice Department for reforms, some police departments are finding it very difficult to implement the inclusion of nonwhite police officers.

The diversity of the police in Ferguson, Missouri, captures the numbers for most police departments in America. Let us verify the composition of the police department there. By the way, the population of Ferguson has changed greatly over the last few decades.

Brookings Research shows that in 1980, the population was largely made up of whites. White folks made up approximately 85 percent. Between 2008 and 2012, the community had changed from 85 percent whites to approximately 67 percent blacks.

From the same report, we deduce that across the United States, 99% of large urban areas with over 20 percent below the federal poverty line, doubled between the years 2000 and 2012.

Such neighborhoods are usually but not always black and Hispanic. The extended recent recession and the snail-speed recovery have not been kind to places like Ferguson. In places such as Ferguson, citizens living below the poverty line have grown to over 25 percent. The unemployment rate has almost tripled from 5 percent in 2000 to approximately 14 percent between 2010 and 2012.

The racial demographics in Ferguson mirrors many areas in the United States. It is another bowl of combinations according to a *USA Today* report which says that in 1970, 99 percent of Ferguson was white. That demographic has changed so much so that whites have decreased to 29 percent. While the population of whites reduced to 29 percent, the police department was nearly at 99.9 percent white. Any thinking person knows that this was/is a brew for explosion someday. These statistics are representative of most police departments in the United States.

Ferguson, Missouri, had 53 police officers during the riot of 2014. Of those 53, 50 were white officers while only three were black.

The chief of police for the department was also white.

It would not be doubtful if the three black officers turned out to be the janitors and gardeners.

Even in other black neighborhoods like Baltimore, most officers are whites. It is not like one is singling out the police for their lack of diversity. Diversity is a bad word in the psyche of this country.

Most ways for doing business in America frown at diversity. From the beginning, unions were formed to keep nonwhites out of the job market. Whether in areas of residence, schools, TV, residents, churches, businesses, you name it . . . there has never been diversity.

Diversity is when some companies filled most of their positions and reserved the receptionist/spokesperson's position for a nonwhite. The attempt to position a nonwhite as the face of an organization is an attempt to create an illusion of diversity.

This same gimmick sometimes is used for advertising purposes today.

To be fair, some of the police chiefs are now making efforts to recruit nonwhite police officers. Especially with the increased animosity between the white police and black communities, some police departments are doubling down on efforts to include nonwhite police officers.

Unfortunately, police chiefs across the nation are finding out the hard way that years of systemic caging of the black folks by any or no excuses, has rendered the pool for the potential nonwhite officers unfit for hire.

NYPD (New York Police Department) Police Commissioner Bill Bratton once confessed that a history of indiscriminate policing tactics that disproportionately targeted black and Latino men has complicated the department's goal of racial parity.

Hear him! "Hiring more nonwhite officers is difficult because so many would-be recruits have criminal records. We have a significant population gap among African American males because so many of them have spent time in jail and, as such, we can't hire them."

Most police departments across the nation would tell you that they are having difficulties recruiting black police officers. This is because most black men's records have been deliberately ruined for minor stuff all across the nation.

Is that a surprise?

If you squeeze the noose on anybody's neck of the woods, you will strangle that neighborhood. Sometimes one wonders if these situations are not deliberately and silently worked out to allow capitalism to thrive.

Imagine this: If every white person with two grams of coke was arrested and incarcerated, if every white person with two grams of cannabis was arrested and incarcerated, and if every white person who shoplifts is arrested and jailed, how many white persons do you expect to be languishing in jails across the nation, let alone be in the various police departments?

That is the truth of the matter. A systemic destruction of the black family. Is there a justification to rubbish the African American family this way?

Yes!

For one, the more black people are tainted with time spent in jail and rendered unfit for the job market, the more job openings you create for other people who are not black.

You may now ask the question, "Who is the police department taking orders from?" Answering that question correctly will begin to make you start seeing the two sides of America's "freedom."

If you start to wonder whether the authorities are working to protect all its citizens or they are protecting some and caging some others for the protection of the protected, then you are beginning to get it when commentators say discrimination is systemic.

There is one thing you cannot miss here: The police are like the media. They do what they are told. Good or bad. They do it while lying to your face. And by the way, like the media, police are good liars too. They take orders and forge the story to suit their purpose.

That is police work.

It's not just police in your neck of the wood but police all over the world.

Like news people, the police all over the world take their orders from somebody. The various police departments across the nation take their marching orders from the mayors and/or the governors who, in turn, take their orders from special interest groups. Special interests are no other than the big corporations of today—the landowners (mercantilists) of yesterday.

Always, almost always, bear that in mind the next time, or anytime, you want to blame the police department. At all times, police officers are carrying out orders from their boss.

The police's primary responsibility is the maintenance of public order, prevention, and detection of crimes in the communities. The police are also responsible to protect the life, liberty, and property of the people. Every modern and fairly populated city worldwide has a need for policing.

The emergence of policing in the United States closely copied and followed the development of policing in England. The landowners had a stronger need for protection of lives and properties.

An institution such as a police force had to be created. Though there was some sort of outfit sanctioned to pass as law enforcers in big cities such as New York, such outfits described as watch systems were composed of community volunteers. Boston was a city with a watch system in 1636 while New York started a watch system in 1658. By 1700, Philadelphia joined the ranks of the night watch. The night watch was not a particularly effective crime control device. Soon, the day watch emerged.

Philadelphia created the first day watch in 1833, and New York instituted a day watch in 1844, a decade later.

You may be perplexed that more than crime, the modern police departments in the South emerged more as a response to the catching and disciplining of runaway slaves than to crime. Therefore, slave catching and disciplining was policing in the South at that time in our history.

So, who is doing the defining of policing? That question needs an answer because some people make up what policing is all about as they move along and that depended on a given circumstance.

Some simply take it that policing was merely catching criminals—sorry—slaves—and holding them down. Policing encompasses the determination of who the unwanted riffraff in the population should be, and then doing what it takes to quarantine them.

What constitutes the "unwanted bad" people of society depends largely on who is defining those terms. In the America of yesteryears, those terms were defined by the mercantile interests—rich landowners—today's multibillion-dollar corporations—who, through taxes and political influence, supports the development and sometimes funding of policing institutions.

The economic interests of the corporations had a greater interest in social control than crime control. The emerging capitalists and indeed today's elites need a mechanism to ensure stable and orderly communities, a workforce, a stable and orderly environment for the conduct of daily businesses.

In those days, the police-type organizations were private and perhaps expensive to run and yet, less effective. Those big-business people thus envisaged to relieve themselves from the costs of protecting their own business and communities, thereby transferring those costs from themselves to the taxpayers.

MORE DETAILS OF EARLY POLICING IN THE SOUTH

While cities in the North had a need to establish police organizations modeled after England to manage increasing crimes, especially crimes against new immigrants and also due to increasing populations, the South was also forming police outfits for almost a different purpose.

The beginning of policing that metamorphosed into the modern police organizations in the South was unsurprisingly referred to as "Slave Patrols." The first such formal slave patrol was created in the Carolina colonies in 1704. The outfit had a few primary functions, all centered on policing black and white slaves.

Their functions included but were not limited to:

(1) protecting properties of the landowners—slaves were property too

(2) chasing down, capturing, and returning to their owners any runaway slave

(3) providing a backbone of organized terror for the landowners so as to deter slave revolts

(4) maintaining discipline and enforcing the pronouncements on slaves who were subject to summary justice—outside of the laws but within the laws of the plantations

You can see that policing revolved around slaves in the early United States. And by common sense, who do you think are the hunted today?

Simple question: Is it any different today? Do you see where some bad apples among some police departments got their modus operandi DNA from, so to speak? Are policing and policies any different in the South today?

Some citizens today are still no different or any better off than the slaves of the 1600s or 1963. After the Civil War—a war fought for property reasons as opposed to what some would want you to buy into as war against slavery—the vigilante-type organizations evolved into the modern Southern police departments of today. They were the metamorphosis of today's police. The same institution used as a means to controlling freed slaves (what you are now) who were now laborers working in a corporation of today or the landowners' agricultural caste system of those years. There is usually a history.

Just like they were enforcing the Jim Crow segregation laws then, so they are enforcing the wishes of the capitalist oligarchs now. They were designed by the laws and used to deny freed slaves equal rights and access to the political system then, just the same way they are used as the masters' hands in caging the freed slaves of today, otherwise referred to as African Americans.

Having read this far, can you comprehend how the press influences the operations of the police? The truth of the matter is that those who control the press are also the controllers of the arms of coercion, directly or indirectly.

The mayors, governors, representatives, senators, etc., are, to a degree, in the pockets of interest groups. The degree may vary. You are likely saying that they are answerable to the electorates. That some of us enjoy the benefits of naïveté sometimes is not by accident.

Police should be able to carry out duties for any of the controllers of the powers of coercion. No questions or suspicions there, but how come the modus operandi of the majority of police departments in the USA are almost scripted? It does not matter who the mayor or governor is, the functions of the police remain the same. Their modus operandi remain the same. Police organizations worldwide are supposed to:

1. Contain criminals
2. Enforce laws
3. Enforce laws even if discriminatory

And that includes enforcing those functions that are inimical to minority freedoms.

Always inimical.

Like the newspeople, the police are scripted.

THE COURTS

From the outside looking in, I saw . . .

The functions of the courts to interpret the laws had never been in doubt. What is in doubt is whether the courts are rubber stamps to the will of the landowners. There are reasons to doubt the courts. The courts' function to interpreting laws include good and bad laws.

The courts have a guideline for interpreting the statutes, and like all our laws, such guidelines have hidden barriers in the setup.

Here is an example: The Thirteenth Amendment abolished slavery with the left hand and reintroduced slavery with the right hand by the amendment to the Thirteenth Amendment. The courts were indirectly charged to oversee who lost their freedoms by the exception in the Thirteenth Amendment. The fear then and now was/is . . . Who were the faces behind the operations of the courts?

It is not news that the courts have been sentencing nonwhites to longer prison terms for the same offenses committed by both whites and nonwhites. It has always been the standard practice, and statistics are available to prove this.

Obviously, the courts are not impartial. The courts have been shaped by the same racist environment that have shaped all other departments in America's existence.

There is a historical precedence to fear what courts might do. There is a fear that a court might interpret statutes to satisfy the majority and/or a few minority.

In the United States and other places, there exists a large number of cases that dealt with the Fugitive Slave Law and their enforcement. Courts have also dealt with other topics that included the ending of the slave trade, criminal prosecutions of slaveholders for mistreatment of slaves, and regulating the expansion of slavery into the territories. The outcomes then would not necessarily be the same today.

That the courts even entertained slave matters is a historical pointer to the times.

The cases represented in the courts at that time raise an array of fundamental constitutional issues. There was the property rights issue, the state's rights issues, and especially the natural law issues. There was the issue of whether the court was part of an independent judiciary among many other issues.

There was the cruel and unusual punishment issue then as it is now, and freedom of religion, among others.

If not for some bad laws passed by Congress that force the courts to follow particular guidelines, the courts in America perhaps would be second to none on earth.

CHAPTER 12

The Prisons:
The American Jails

———

JAILS ARE GENERALLY BUILT TO house bad people. They are built in every country. In some countries, they house political enemies too. In some countries like Denmark, prisons serve as a place to reform behaviors not punish. In many countries, prisons are used to cage indecent people, thus protecting the general population.

In the United States, the prisons serve all the above functions . . . and much more. If you really think about it, there are statistical conclusions from which one can draw. Like, the prisons were built in the first place to house dangerous and/or feared angry black males.

It costs less to educate a person than incarcerate him/her in the United States. The benefits to the society of educating an individual are many. For one, you create many good people instead of bad people.

However, statistical evidence presents a different intention of those in charge. You can deduce the intentions from some or most of the legislated practices. Why choose an option to build more prisons than schools? You build more prisons because there is the intention to fill them up.

It will not be bad or racist if the prison population is representative of the American population. Racial and ethnic disparities are an unacceptable but defining characteristics of our prison system.

You probably have heard or read somewhere the United States' prison statistics compared to the world's prison population. It will be nice to read it one more time.

U.S. incarceration rates by race: FIG 10

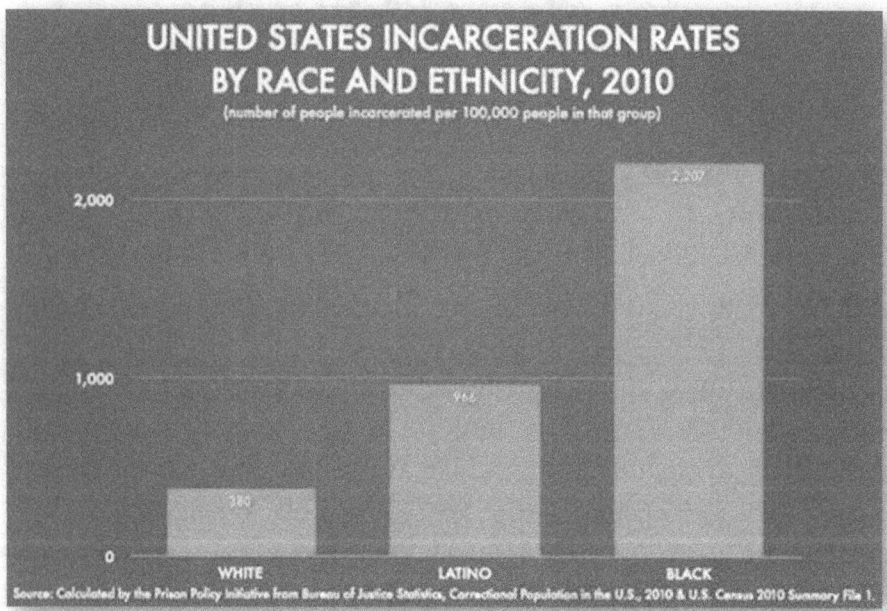

The average incarceration rate in the United States is approximately 720 persons per every 100,000 residents. This is far higher than any other country on earth. As if that is not bad enough, black incarceration rates hover at 2,200 persons for every 100,000 residents.

These incarceration rates did not happen because all of a sudden black people suddenly woke up one morning and became criminals. It is so because policy makers decided they wanted more people incarcerated. That more black people are used to populate the prisons to capacity was no accident either.

More people does not equal more white people. It means more black people, notwithstanding that black folks are only 12 percent of the general population. Do you even wonder why the black general population has been steady at 12 percent?

Why do you think that incarceration, which is costlier, is a chosen option of policy makers?

You may listen to any intellectual of your liking, you may read fine doctors of economics, yet they will not tell you some of the obvious truths. If they did, their meanings are hidden in chosen words hard to understand. A few things that are "open secrets" are:

1. Incarceration protects jobs for persons not incarcerated
2. Incarceration engenders the systemic reduction/destruction of African America families
3. Incarceration in America is a tool to promote and maintain the livelihoods of the middle class and others. The more African Americans that are incarcerated, the harder the job opportunities there are for them.

You might reason logically and question the economic sense in sidelining millions of people through discrimination. Many economists have asked that question too.

The thing is this: The rich landowners have figured the answer a long time ago. It was called divide and conquer. The middle class is used to subjugating the poor for the landowners to stay afloat—on top.

Does this even start to lay a foundation to understanding the dilemma black folks are in? Not at all. Not when there is a connivance among the various people in places, as in the media, courts, and policy making.

Blacks are thieves, loud, idiots, and criminals. They are also senseless, don't know how to act, and are welfare recipients, among others. Those are a few reasons they must be incarcerated. Even if the stereotypes were true, what people would sustain self if caged like African Americans?

It is a bafflement that sane and happy African Americans exist in America today.

There is no reason why the incarceration rate, especially that of African Americans in the United States, is highest in the world. Even the incarceration in a few states like Louisiana, Mississippi, Oklahoma, Georgia, and Texas is greater than the world's leading incarceration countries.

The state of Louisiana is often looked at as having the highest incarceration rates. It is a state in the thick with black folks. Why should anyone be surprised? You should not be surprised about Louisiana. Louisiana is the affirmation of the intent and purposes why the United States has the highest incarceration rates because of her large black incarceration rates.

Who cares? No one cares. If anyone cared, they'd do something about it.

It is black lives. It is, perhaps, not a priority.

All these did not occur by accident. They were by design. This is an issue not talked about until President Obama made it an issue in his last years in office.

Consider this: The five states with the lowest incarceration rates in the United States are Vermont, Maine, Rhode Island, New Hampshire, and North Dakota. You may want to check the black population in these states in order to figure out why these states have lower incarceration rates.

UNDERSTANDING THE AMENDMENT TO THE FOURTH AMENDMENT

Observing as a layman . . .

On occasions when you are pulled over or stopped, frisked, and questioned on the streets by the police, perhaps you felt you were not allowed to walk away from the officer. If you have not been formally detained or arrested, the officer cannot stop you from walking away. You can ask the officer if you are being arrested. If not, you can simply walk away or drive away.

STOP!

That scenario works well . . . if you are white.

If you are a nonwhite person, the above does not apply, even though it is supposed to. Do not walk away, especially if you are black. You might not live to tell your side of the story. All those caricatures of the black man, put out there by the media, affect the police too. They too are human. They too are scared for their lives. They are doing a job capitalism has offered them.

Do not forget that the officer is a product of the society—American society—and the society was and still is built on capitalism. At this moment, aren't you confident we can use the words *capitalism* and *racism* interchangeably?

The officer might simply say that you refused arrest. You probably have seen a black man get shot on a video. Perhaps, you have watched a video of a child getting shot. If you have not seen one on TV news, do a little research. Police departments are not required to release data on how many civilians are shot by officers each year, and many don't.

Many police officers lose their lives on duty too each year. They have families as well. But they must do the job assigned to them by the oligarchs and for which they swore to do.

There is a better and more polite way to converse with an officer. Remember that you have to leave each encounter *alive*.

Simply ask, "Can I go now?" or "Am I under arrest?" If the officer refuses to allow you to leave, an arrest has just been made.

You may think that you have not done anything illegal, but that is not the problem here. Whether the arrest is legal or illegal depends on a large part on whether the officer has what is called "probable cause." So, anytime, anywhere, any moment, a police officer pulls you over, the issue is not what you may or may not have done.

Just have the mind-set that for all situations, the officer has a "probable cause." Some people might advise that to understand this fact, especially by black folks, might lead to less rancor and perhaps save black lives. It is a maybe or maybe not.

Aren't you wondering whether black people got a reprieve then when they acknowledged persons of authority with a "yes sir" or a "yes ma'am"?

The amendment to the Fourth Amendment gives the police this right. The amendment simply says that if the officer believes he has "probable cause" to search and arrest, he may as well do that.

Before you read further, what other amendment to an amendment comes to mind? If you think about it, this amendment can be a twin to the Thirteenth Amendment. The only thing separating both twins is time.

The Fourth Amendment was intended to enforce the notion that your home is your castle and is secure from unreasonable searches and seizures of property by the government. The Fourth Amendment, it was thought, would protect against arbitrary arrests. It is also the basis of the law regarding search warrants, stop-and-frisk, wiretaps, and other forms of surveillance.

However, the amendment to Fourth Amendment says that "the right of the people to be secure in their persons, houses, papers, and effects, against unreasonable searches and seizures, shall not be violated, and no warrants shall issue, but upon probable cause, supported by oath or affirmation, and particularly describing the place to be searched, and the persons or things to be seized"

It has the same characteristics as the Thirteenth Amendment. With the right hand, it gave you freedoms, and with the left, it guarantees how those freedoms are a mirage.

Do you see a problem here—the amendment to the Fourth Amendment and stand-your-ground laws? These laws all reeks of racism. If you don't see the racism, then an explanation here is fine.

How do you think blacks are perceived in the United States? Some TV stations refer to black men as thugs. Even the police refer to black men they have killed as thugs. Since the media has done such a good job of making monsters of black men, are you then shocked that such laws as amendments to another amendment are manufactured to give cover to law enforcers while fishing for the monsters?

Many legal scholars have pointed out the connections between reasonableness and "probable cause" vis-à-vis race, as problematic. Nonwhites, African Americans in particular, have been demonized in popular culture as a group that is violence-prone and mostly dangerous.

It is a simple logic. First, give it a bad name . . . then kill it. That is where the stand-your-ground laws come in. Can you now see how the racist laws are woven into America's fabric? As it was in the beginning, so it is today. These laws were motivated by fear of a group of people.

Sociologists are quick to talk about nature and nurture. While the greater society is nudging black men into crimes, sociologists keep reminding the general population that the fear of the black males is widely shared, sometimes unconsciously (some white medical students unconsciously believe that black men tolerate pain better, so less painkillers are administered).

Not all Americans are obviously listening.

If they were listening, the "probable cause" and stand-your-ground laws would not be reasonable. As it stands now, in the minds of some

Americans, the fear of all black males, and the frequent use of all means including deadly force, is "reasonable."

It seems like every selective far-reaching legislation and the enforcement of such laws is reasonable . . . as long as it is happening to nonwhites.

"Probable cause" can also justify a warrantless search. The "probable cause" clause is a very powerful tool for the police in some neighborhoods. It was such a powerful tool in New York City that it became one of the platforms to run for political office. Mayor De Blasio has since complied with the modifications to the stop-and-frisk practices.

Stop and frisk, per se, is not the issue. The use of this method in selected communities and its selective application is the issue. There are other instances where "stop and search" is used, especially when public safety is threatened.

If you are nonwhite, it is not news that there is animosity, lack of trust, and suspicion between the police and especially black men. If it is news, you may be one of the privileged ones—white, rich, or perhaps middle class.

You can be rich and black, but the richness that possessed you to buy and drive a Mercedes-Benz or BMW while black is enough "probable cause" for an officer to pull you over. Capitalism, by the way it has been set to work in the United States and, by extension, the way it was meant to work for the poor and black folks, makes it easy for the police to have suspicions.

You are set up to be poor. How, then, are you riding/driving a Bentley or a Ferrari? Do you now blame the police? Can you not see that driving while black and rich is against capitalism?

You are not supposed to participate in capitalism. Therefore, there is a "probable cause," and you must explain. You are lucky if your record is clean, but if it is dirty, you may go from the comfort of your Mercedes to the precinct's (police station) lockup.

You have been arrested and convicted; your record is messed up. Once your record is messed up, your chance of getting a job is doomed. Your chance of getting into the police is perhaps zero. Realistically, your chance of getting into private security is zilch.

Whether that is the "intent" in the first place is a reasonable assumption. So, some of the many "hidden" reasons to arrest young black men are:

1. Arrest to provide arrest records. Might lead to conviction of yet another black man. Keep them down.
2. Stop and frisk to increase the probability that the police would find something and you get arrested.
3. Predatory policing: If you stop white drivers and search for illegal drugs, the probability of finding something is not zero. If you do not pull white drivers off the road, the probability of finding drugs is zero. It is common sense and those whose intent it has been to keep blacks and other people of color down knows this. The chances that white landowners/rich men of today would be pulled off the roadway or caught with drugs and/or sentenced to jail is near zero. They are hardly on the roadways, and when they are, they are chauffeur driven. Sometimes, they are helicoptered from one city to another. It might sound funny and perhaps far-fetched, but there are no police in the air to pull them over or down.

Some researchers find that black neighborhoods are overpoliced. That is true. Following the arguments above, the overpoliced neighborhoods are most likely to provide "raw materials" for the prisons.

As it was yesterday, so it is today.

More than 60 percent of those incarcerated are blacks. Another 17 percent are Hispanics. Blacks make up 12–13 percent of the general population. Some TV pundits are so good at making some racist comments. One of which is that blacks fill the prisons because blacks commit more crimes. Another one is that blacks need more policing because blacks kill blacks.

Does it surprise you that like mental slavery, they are not self-aware that they are racist? What these racist pundits would not say is that these communities are the way they are because of hidden barriers and the setup.

The hope is, somebody would have to remind these pundits that the same statistics of who kills their kind is mathematically and incrementally proportionate in every neighborhood, including white ones. We don't see overpolicing and/or predatory policing in all the neighborhoods.

The hope is that next time, they could follow their arguments with— black people have been denied jobs more than whites, black people have been kept down since slavery more than whites, black people are systemically impoverished more than whites, and that the black population has been under control since the introduction of the amendment to the Thirteenth Amendment more than whites.

4. To keep jobs for middle-class America. The impoverishment of nonwhites and their ultimate incarceration create jobs for the middle class.

When you adopt a child, common sense says you must treat that child as your own, or at least as a human. When you agree to bring a child to your house for the purposes of babysitting, you are required to give that baby your undivided attention. You do not bring a child into your house and abandon that child. If and when you abandon that child, there is every likelihood that that child is going to resent you.

Smart parents know what not to do while raising a child. Companies know what to do to get the best from their employees. When employees are treated badly, the first thing you notice is high employee turnover. And that is just the beginning. You do not fail woefully in your bid to bring up a child and hope to receive kisses from that child.

Even if you messed up bringing up a child, you do not rely on hope that the child will be a forgiving type. You do not resort to incarceration to cage the child. You do not bring down the child while pretending to be on the child's side.

That America cannot own up to the evil some of our grandfathers perpetuated is painful. That America still deems it fit to continue the perpetuation of injustices of the 1850s and pretend they are doing themselves a favor is nothing but denial.

When you position a group of peoples to be poor and weak through the hidden barriers in the setup, how long do we hope to sustain this?

One thing is certain. It cannot be forever.

We pretend not to know that the only thing standing between people of color and the economic meal of a lifetime is the systemic embroidery of racial laws into America's system of laws.

And it is holding very well today.

Just like slavery, this was and still is systemic and intentionally woven into America's fabric of life. There are those that still deny that racism doesn't exist anymore. Left to those same people, they would deny that slavery never happened.

CHAPTER 13

Economics of Capitalism

You may have noticed the insinuation that the survival of capitalism is dependent on the creation of poor people and more of them, some middle class (the fewer the better), while the corporation keeps amassing more wealth.

If you looked at history, you will confirm the above. That was and still is the way it was set up to function and the way it is practiced in the United States.

Economists, year after year, postulate that the economies of the world (perhaps, global trade) is producing more middle class across the globe. If you look at it closely, you start to question the definition of middle class.

Who, exactly, is middle class in America today? Perhaps, middle class in the United States is a family with a house, two or three cars, and an annual income of approximately $100K.

And a family living somewhere near the Sahara Desert, in a mud house (suitable for the hot desert), with two or three camels and a large farm is middle class. The point here is that there is no universally recognized definition of middle class.

The poor class must be milked to feed the middle class so as to calm what otherwise would have turned out to be some dormant grievances waiting to explode. Remember that the middle class is the creation of the capitalists to provide protection for self. The upper class cannot afford to anger the middle class because the middle class does the protecting of the upper class through the departments of police, courts, media, etc.

Michael Reich, the economist, could not have said any better when he beautifully wrote in one of his articles, *"The Economics of Racism"*:

> *Thus, racism is likely to take firm root in a society that breeds an individualistic and competitive ethos. In general, blacks provide a convenient and visible scapegoat for problems that actually derive from the institutions of capitalism. As long as building a real alternative to capitalism does not seem feasible to most whites, we can expect that identifiable and vulnerable scapegoats will prove functional to the status quo. These non-economic factors thus neatly dovetail with the economic aspects of racism discussed earlier in their mutual service to the perpetuation of capitalism.*

Statistics abound of salary inequality (income inequality) between white and black workers. Blacks are generally paid less. Women too. Common sense has it that if you pay $4 to produce something where you will normally pay $10, the profit would be higher.

Therefore, it would make economic sense that under normal circumstances, slavery was used for economic advancement of some people. If that was the case, how come blacks are not getting the jobs because they are still paid less? Are they, no longer, a source of cheap labor?

It defies logic. You can safely say that racism is not strictly economic. It was and still is. It was very prioritized for the enhancement of capitalism. It is hard to see, but once you see the hidden barriers in the setup, you will see it in its evilness.

Michael Reich draws the same conclusion in the above quoted article *". . . a full assessment of the importance of racism for capitalism would probably conclude that the primary significance of racism is not strictly economic. The simple economics of racism does not explain why many workers seem to be so vehemently racist, when racism is not in their economic self-interest. In non-economic ways, racism helps to legitimize inequality, alienation, and powerlessness—legitimization that is necessary for the stability of the capitalist system as a whole."*

I believe that in all societies, there should be no need to suggest or conceal an obvious truth, the fact that a substantial amount of income inequality is inevitable in a capitalist society. It has always been so.

Riches and poverty are not supposed to be equitably distributed among all citizens. It should be distributed proportionately according to skills and time invested. To that, I have no qualms with capitalism.

There are, however, serious issues when a group of citizens are directly targeted so that the ability to participate in capitalism is contained. This is the setup in the United States of America.

Capitalism, when you comprehend the mechanisms and its impact, you will also come to the same conclusions that capitalism is bad for African Americans and poor white Americans or that capitalism is the new slavery for both poor whites and unprivileged blacks. That was the way it has always been.

You remember the explanation and transformation of white slavery?

The white slaves became middle class, the landowners became the upper class (the rich 10 percent), and the suppressed blacks became the freedmen. A freedman or freedwoman is a former slave who has been released from slavery, usually by legal means. Historically, slaves were freed either by manumission—granted freedom by their owner or emancipation—granted freedom as part of a larger group.

Capitalism is the name of the power structure that currently dominates all human society and which has done so for so many years. It is a system based on ecological and social exploitation for the profit of the wealthy few worldwide.

A dictionary.com Web site defined capitalism as an economic system in which investment in and ownership of the means of production, distribution, and exchange of wealth is made and maintained chiefly by private individuals or corporations, especially as contrasted to cooperatively or state-owned means of wealth.

The Web site Capitalism.org defines it as a social system based on the recognition of individual rights, including property rights, in which all property is privately owned. Under *capitalism,* the state is separated from economics (production and trade), just like the state is separated from religion. *Capitalism* is the system of laissez-faire.

What is bad in the above definitions? Absolutely nothing. People should love capitalism. I grew up in capitalism. We were mostly schooled in capitalism in capitalistic societies. I am an enthusiast of capitalism. But no one taught us the history and the intents of entrepreneurial capitalism. Entrepreneurial capitalism, as practiced in the United States, entrenches systemic racism. Its manipulative intent in the United States is not equitable.

That is what should not be cherished in capitalism.

Now, you see why capitalists have a bad moral reputation. People see capitalists/capitalism as bad because this is an economic theory based on self-interest, greed, and subjugation of blacks in America.

Entrepreneurial capitalism, as practiced in America, is nothing but modern-day slavery.

There are some authors who have opined that the best capitalism is the entrepreneurial practice type. Perhaps they did not, could not, or they outrightly refused to see the racism inherent in this type of capitalism. Some capitalists are just plain jerks who continue to think that this economic system—entrepreneurial capitalism—is some newfound religion that must be practiced worldwide. Some believe in this system, so much so, that they are rigid in their thinking. Some countries have learned a lot from American capitalism.

Unfortunately, the rulers in most oil-producing states have become oligarchs too and have copied the American weapon of slavery in their own nations. They have subjugated the regions where oil is found and produced and have the citizens in such regions reduced to beggars. They did this so that the people in the oil-producing regions will be so impoverished they cannot rise in protests.

There are some unrepentant capitalists. I can now also see the intents of those people who imbibed and practiced capitalism American style. Some are not good moral humans. They lack love and compassion and all sense of equity lost to a type of greed—the bad type. Some are simply heartless racists or tribalists.

You may have seen a history where continents were invaded and plundered, looted and killed; that was the name of the game. You can now understand why.

There is no need paying any attention or qualms where the rich are stereotyped as greedy and heartless. A little greed is good and motivational. The draw to invest is the large amount of earnings we hope to garner through our investments.

Mostly, everyone wants to be rich. At least, I do. When people use their brains, I love that. When people contribute to society, we cherish that. We want to contribute to society too. Perhaps, we want to make money, and lots of it too. There is absolutely nothing wrong in building wealth.

What is absolutely unacceptable is the entrenched and systemic racism that capitalism brings with it—the American-type capitalism.

How can people not see through the lies? That some of the rich are seen as parasites, that feed off the sweat of others also did not bother me. I used to think that if I am susceptible to be taken advantage of, that means I am less smart.

Perhaps that is the way most capitalists think too. It is not right to think that way unless the facts are not taught in schools. Why should it be taught in schools when the schools' curriculum is dictated by the capitalists?

But the rich are not smarter. They just weave their greed into the system, and we have legalized racism. If not for the infusion of racism, if not the denial of privileges to nonwhite Americans, capitalism itself is not bad, nor are the capitalists.

Capitalism is good. Very good. Racism is bad. Very bad. Racism, otherwise known as white supremacy, in the United States, is sinful.

Capitalism comes in various forms. Oligarchic capitalism is the type that is prevalent in much of Latin and South America, Africa and the Middle East.

Some authors would tell you that this is to be avoided because it is designed to promote the interests of the ruling few. Personally, I do not see the difference between this and the type practiced in United Sates. If anything, capitalism was copied from the United States.

The bottom line of both practices in the United States and other places is to aggregate riches for the richest few. If there is any measurable difference—that difference is the missing racism in other places, which makes such capitalism even better than the type practiced in the United States.

But somehow, capitalists still find a way to blindfold the poor people.

One very important thing about capitalism is competition. Competition does not allow your competitor to lag behind. You lag, you lose. You lag, you are out of the competition. State guided capitalism has a penchant to be consistently behind the competition because governments are slow to respond to innovation. They make too many mistakes in managing an economy. Despite all of the above and in spite of some of the failures of corporate institutions and instances of corporate greed, capitalism without racism still remains a good thing.

Centuries of slavery and almost a century and half after the abolition of slavery, America and/or American-type capitalism is still very far from achieving genuine equality for all, the black race being the most devastated. Though there has been a number of advances achieved economically here and there, the position and participation of black Americans in our capitalism remains one of clear disadvantage.

Though capitalism has not benefited the African American community as it should from the beginning, there is no denying that if and when the hidden barriers in the setup are removed and if attitudes change, the beneficiary, to a greater extent, will be the American economy.

Blacks, whether native-born or immigrants, should be able to participate in capitalism if the hidden barriers are taken out and not used to make an argument for the success of black immigrants and the castigation of native-born African Americans.

CHAPTER 14

The Black Immigrant Argument

———

BY THE WAY, IMMIGRANTS HAVE choices. They can stay or they can leave. Black immigrants too have choices between two locations. This choice is highly motivating. An average immigrant's dream is to rise up to a middle-class status in their home country, and achieving that status while in America makes it cheaper. Middle class is defined as owning a house, two or three cars, and a large farm or a fairly salivating salary.

The black immigrant argument is simply that black immigrants are doing better than native blacks in the United States. This is the sort of argument those who want to divide and conquer make. They seek some statistics to buttress their statements. They use variables like scores in school tests, holding down jobs, unemployment levels, and other variables.

By the way, immigrants are also doing better than some whites—the poor ones.

Immigrants are so water thirsty—so to speak—they see mirages at every few feet. Give them water and they will drink. Immigrants are a bunch of the most motivated group of people. They can be whites, blacks, or Hispanics and the other 99 shades of blacks.

An immigrant is one who specifically immigrates to another country to capitalize and exploit available opportunities. That is the intent and purpose and the driving force behind immigration. Comparing any immigrant group to virtually whites, blacks, Hispanics, or any native-born group is like comparing the most ambitious and hungriest people with a people who have food leftovers every day. In fact, there is no basis for comparison. This is to say nothing of whatever skills, education, and wealth a particular immigrant group may bring to bear.

Always bear in mind that in America someone will always be the villain. Understand that America made Italians the villain, just like the Irish. It has always been the fashion here to make a group the villain. Some groups just have to be the villain.

The argument that the immigrant black is faring better is what it is, the perpetuation of that same sentiment of—someone has to be the villain.

Is it America's fault? The system has been rigged that way so that at every turn there is a villain. American native blacks just happened to be the group that carried the severity of the hate and racism. It was so designed. In all things, the systemic strangulation is tight and still tightening.

You have to research and accept as truth what happened to blacks postslavery. It will be nice if you research during slavery too. How many groups of peoples can even come out of those periods and remain sane?

It is very hard for some people to fathom, much less to accept, what has happened to black people in this country postslavery. Most countries had slaves. Brazil, Jamaica, Haiti, Saudi Arabia all had slaves. When you mention any country, the answer is probably yes—they engaged in slavery. Of all the countries that engaged in the sinful act of slavery, none continued caging the freedmen and freedwomen like America does.

The Jim Crow laws were specifically legislated for that purpose. The Klan emerged to remind the polity that white supremacy is the boss. They tended the gates to freedom and financial freedom.

None of these other countries saw fit to use entrepreneurial capitalism to discriminate against their black populace.

Part of sticking it to the African Americans is to incarcerate their men, creating households with no father figure. Where a father did exist, they could not be gainfully employed because the forces for coercion had been used to smear his character. They now have bad records for misdemeanors/crimes for which the white race is not even policed. Even where the white folks are arrested and jailed, they come out with the job market waiting to engage them. The privilege is loud and deafening.

What happens in the majority of households without a father figure? Below, I reproduce some statistics from a Web site—First Things First. Before you read the information, let's ask ourselves some of these questions:

"Where are the black men?"
Answer: "In jails."
Ask: "Why?"
Answer: "They stole a loaf of bread from the grocery store."
"Why?"
Answer: "They were hungry."
"Why can't they work?"
Answer: "They cannot work because their records were messed up and where the records are clean, they still would not get jobs."

Do you see a revolving door of no escape that the majority of blacks in the United States must pass through?

Here are the statistics:

Hamilton County Marriage Report/Harris Interactive 2005

African Americans are the most unpartnered group in America. Census figures show that 43 percent of African Americans have never married compared to 25 percent of whites who have never married. About four out of every 10 African American men and women had never been married, the highest proportion of any racial category—**US Census 2003.**

Compared to 94 percent of whites, only 80 percent of African Americans in Hamilton County say that they expect to be married for life.

Nineteen percent of African Americans in Hamilton County believe that marriage is "outmoded" compared to 9 percent of whites who feel the same way.

Nearly one-half (48 percent) of all African American families were married. Forty-three percent of all African American families were maintained by women with no spouse present.

A larger proportion of African American married (couple) families (8 percent) were poor compared to white families (3 percent). Poverty was highest in families maintained by women with no spouse present, 35 percent for African American families compared to 19 percent for white families.

Among women, African Americans and Hispanics had the highest percentage of being separated, 6 percent and 5 percent respectively. Research has shown that African American and Hispanic women are more likely to remain separated without getting a legal divorce than are women of other groups.

A comparatively high percentage of African American grandparents were living in the same household as their grandchildren (8 percent) compared to whites (2 percent). More than half of the African American grandparents report that they are responsible for the basic needs of their grandchildren.

From the web page of Unmarried Equality, we find that, in 2005, 69.5 percent of all births outside of marriage occurred to black women, 63.3 percent of births outside of marriage occurred to American Indians or Alaskan native woman, and 47.9 percent occurred to Hispanic women, compared with 25.4 percent for non-Hispanic white women and 16.2 percent for Asian or Pacific Islander women (Child Trends DataBank, 2007).

Black children are significantly less likely than other children to be living with two married parents. In 2006, 35 percent of black children were living with two parents, compared with 84 percent of Asian children, 76 percent of non-Hispanic white children, and 66 percent of Hispanic children (Child Trends DataBank, 2007).

Approximately 30.9 percent of blacks are married, compared to 69.1 percent unmarried, while 7.5 percent of the married population is black, compared to 19.8 percent of the unmarried population (U.S. Census Bureau. American Community Survey: 2005–2007).

The above is reflective of black communities nationwide.

This statistical data challenge our self-image as Americans. The black experience in the United States is enough to ruin the image and self-worth of a country.

The placement of native blacks at the lower end of the economic ladder is so systemic that mere ambition and motivation cannot suddenly move native blacks to doing better than immigrants.

The American native black has been caged. There is nowhere to go—except perhaps to jails. The immigrant blacks enjoy the same predicament with a difference—they have a place to return to where they would not be singled out to suffer the indignities of racist capitalism.

Until the cage is thrown wide open, all blacks—native and sons of black immigrants—would suffer the same economic, unemployment, and judicial humiliation under the so-called home of capitalism. The immigrant blacks are not shielded from the same racism meted to other blacks.

The one big difference is that the immigrant blacks can return to their home country if they feel their sojourn in America is over. The other difference is, it takes less resources to be a success and become a middle-class member in almost all of the immigrants' original countries.

The argument that immigrant blacks are doing better in any sphere of American life is a knee-jerk reaction by the same promoters of racial divisiveness, profiling, higher incarceration, and economic blockade of native blacks.

Such methods and arguments are just a cover for the justification of the near-total destruction of black families in the United States. It is therefore a natural and, ultimately, a cheap reaction to appeal to the nonexisting success myth of the black immigrant. The use of the divide-and-conquer tactic is obviously still in vogue.

Ultimately, those making the argument for black immigrants and against native blacks are seeking justification for the immoral deeds of their forefathers, while at the same time nudging the native blacks to acknowledge and accept personal failures and show less self-pity.

The truth of the matter is: No race can survive the injustices that were systemically inflicted on native blacks. That the native blacks survive today is a marvel and a revelation that they were built to last.

CHAPTER 15

Unions as Hidden Barriers

———

WHILE SLAVERY WAS GETTING ERADICATED by Proclamation, radical changes needed to alleviate and mitigate systemic domination were not pursued. Instead, plans were put in place to perpetuate more crimes against the so-called freed people.

It was a freedom only on paper.

While radical changes to ensure that true freedoms were not pursued, worse things happened. In the same Thirteenth Amendment where freedom for the slaves was proclaimed, a hidden barrier existed. It was an exception that would confiscate the freed and grandsons of the freed into the slammer. A slave or a prisoner—which is worse?

If you put on your thinking cap, this exception was to lubricate the machinery that guaranteed that convicts as prisoners would replace slavery and slaves.

The question that should have been asked then and now was/is *who was making the laws, who was the executioner, who were the jury?* They were the few landowners and those working on their behalf. They can make any law. They can make bad laws.

Not only could they make bad laws, they did. Such laws are responsible for the United States becoming the best at creating super-rich people at the expense of very poor people. Inequality, also, in the

United States is the worst in the industrialized world. This is so because there are radical hidden barriers to economic well-being or upgrades for nonwhites.

They can otherwise make laws that could turn the governments into fishers of the black man. And a government did just that with the three-strikes law.

As a result of the three-strikes law, our prisons were overcrowded with prisoners, many of whom have a third strike for a minor offense such as marijuana possession. It destroys families and is helping to bankrupt every level of government even as the prisoners were used as slave labor.

More radical steps were taken to box in the freed slaves. First was the formation of unions. It was a whites-only club.

Unions, contrary to popular belief that they emerged to protect workers, were formed to perpetuate discrimination. They were set up to help protect white jobs and interests. *All* white jobs and interests. It is still so today, even if you see some tokenism here and there.

Think for a minute. The law of supply and demand dictates the determination of prices. We also know that the cheaper a product, the greater its demand in most cases. We know that blacks, if hired, were paid 55 percent–60 percent of what whites were paid.

You may then think that since capitalism was all about competition, the cheaper labor would prevail. You would think that more black workers would be hired. When it comes to capitalism masked in racism, the law of supply and demand and determination of price are all trumped.

If roles were reversed, would black folks give their jobs to whites? Perhaps that was a rhetorical question. If capitalism was practiced precisely following all economic concepts—not racism—perhaps the need for incarcerating so many people would be like other industrialized countries, or better.

Racism was very important. It was a weapon. Obviously, capitalism was very important. It was a weapon, and it means exactly the same as the sentence preceding this one—racism was very important.

And the weapon was used well and badly. The way you see it today depends on which side you are on and what yoke you are burdened with today.

Racism factored well into the distribution of income and wealth among rich landowners who were the emerging 1 percent capitalists and also the middle class of America. Racism is the reason why most blacks are quarantined in big cities and in tiny spaces of land while the land grab was ongoing.

Perhaps, it was reasoned, that the tinier the land space (neighborhoods) black folks were quarantined in, the better and the easier it is to overpolice. You see, racism benefits owners of houses in the ghetto. They have the money. They build the houses and charge whatever rent they want. Let's not even get into rent stabilization here.

You have no choice.

Meanwhile, the same apartment with same facilities in less dense areas are cheaper in rent, and that is where the middle class lives.

America was not always a racist country. America used to be a place for the rich landowners and laborers. The laborers were white and were later joined by blacks. The laborers were poorly paid and badly treated. There was no middle class.

The creation of a middle class from a pool of the white slaves/laborers was an afterthought. It was a reaction to an insurgency in today's Haiti. It was a divide-and-conquer tactic.

There was a revolution in Haiti. The laborers succeeded in gaining their freedom. For the revolution to have succeeded, they had to maim, kill, and hang the majority of the rich landowners.

America's rich landowners heard the news. They, naturally were worried but worse, they were scared nearly to death. To the landowners, that was no revolution. It was an insurgency. They were not about to let that happen to them in America—then or ever.

Herein lies the logic that would lead to a framework for what was to become the United States of America—the land of the "free."

They devised a tactic. That revolution or as the landowners deemed it—insurgency—was merely the pretext for building a massive counter-insurgency apparatus—the resulting white middle class.

The landowners feared that an insurgency with such smart planners made up of laborers would be one hell of a bunch of angry fighters to contain. What the landowners did then was the ultimate "learn faster than your foe or die," was, in my opinion, counterinsurgency. It was a fear then that is still perpetuated today.

The *us against them* tactic was thus created, and the white supremacy ideology was just the icing on the cake sold to white folks who then were allowed to pay off their masters so that they could become free.

Black slaves were not given that "privilege."

The *we against them* tactic is still very much in play today. If you cannot understand it, listen to the major TV networks. You will notice how they frame the news events.

Notice how they describe the things a white man does and be discerning to notice how they frame the same acts if a black man.

Race and ethnicity, class or gender, and even sexuality were all staple ingredients in the determination of who we are and where we belong. America started from the beginning by categorizing its citizens.

These were/are the benchmarks for your social being, from which all a group's economic practices and political policies create your type of the American citizen.

Racism is such a powerful tool to do bad deeds. The powers are felt in all facets of our social, economic, political, and even in our religious surroundings, with such significant meaning on a national scale.

Racism, also, has major consequences for individuals and groups in terms of successes and well-being. Almost always, racism as can be observed in America, defines how some groups perceive themselves socially, economically, and politically.

Here are a few examples:

During the New Orleans flood disaster, when people of color accessed some food in damaged and flooded stores, the major media described them as "looters," "thugs," and "thieves." However, when the same behavior was exhibited by white males, the same major media described the act as "finders' keepers."

It was and still is looting vs. finding for black and white persons, respectively. White people do not loot, they find, according to America's media.

When a Kenyan gunman killed students, he was described as a terrorist. When an American white male killed many little children in Sandy Hook Elementary School in Newtown, Connecticut, the perpetrator was described as insane. The Sparks Middle School in Nevada suffered a similar type of shooting assault by a white person and had the same media spin.

With investigations drawn from data of news reports, there were over 20 deadly school shootings in about 2 years following the Sandy Hook incident.

Sometimes, the media declares the shooters insane way ahead of the doctors.

Do you see word manipulation? America's media is expected to make black people look as the stereotypes they—the media—has portrayed since their existence.

Differentiating Terrorists vs Insanity.

Insanity, here, implies a suspect's inability to understand their actions when they performed such actions. An American cable channel, East Africa Region, had to issue an apology to the Kenyans shortly after Mr. Obama's visit to that country in July 2015. America's media was earlier portraying the country as a hotbed of terrorism even though the same terrorist events were happening in the United States.

Have you noticed how peaceful black protesters led by a senator or by a member of the House of Representatives would be referred to as "thugs and looters" while whites doing the same—or worse—were referred to as "civil unrest or civil disobedience"?

The words—*angry, tribal, thuggery, scary*, among others—are subtly and constantly infused into the daily narratives of the black man.

Some media houses will go further. They most often accuse the police of doing nothing when protesters are mostly nonwhites. They tend to be more interested in properties (corporate properties) than the protesters' lives. And they broadcast these incidents on "live TV" to mostly a white audience.

Accusing the police of "doing nothing" means many things. It can mean that the police are not beating, arresting, and not excluding the execution of the monsters parading as protesters. If it is mostly black protesters, they could care less; they care for their pets more.

The last Baltimore, Maryland, and Ferguson, Missouri, protests were good examples. The summary execution of protesters could easily have happened but for a female mayor who had the milk of a mother flowing in her. There was not a single black man killed in the protests that happened in Baltimore, Maryland. The price for freedom of speech has cost the black folks an arm, a leg, and many heads.

The media knowingly and consciously does this. It is the process to keep racism alive. Do not forget that the media houses are owned and run by the rich landowners whose laborers are the middle class doing the masters' bidding. This is how subtle racism has been planted.

First, they find words to skew a story, and then sell it. The majority of mankind has a mind that is frail so we—mostly the white populace—suck it up.

According to a 2015 Forbes Global 2000 list, America's largest media in terms of revenue are Comcast, The Walt Disney Company, 21st Century Fox, Time Warner, CBS Corporation, and Viacom.

Still on perception, if you were a geography student, no, if you have ever looked up a map, you will conclude that North America is bigger than Africa. You will conclude that China is smaller than Greenland too. But why was this lie readily accepted?

While some technical reasons might be advanced for these distortions, it is simply an ideological assumption to manipulate in order to change the way we see the world. It is a fabrication to present the lands where people of color dwell to be tiny and less consequential. It is the manipulation of visuals.

It is racist. It is that same continuation of *mine is better and bigger than yours*. It was/is the perpetuation of racism.

The truth was and still is—*Africa is three times bigger than North America. China is four times bigger than Greenland,* and *South America is bigger than Greenland.*

If a people would blatantly lie like the above, what other truths and lies are they perpetrating today? Superiority? If you have to lie over minor things like previously mentioned, you can be anything, but superiority is not one of them. It feels and looks like an attempt to cover inadequacies.

Racism was the creation of the rich white landowners. It was built in, in principle. It is an unspoken built-in concept. The richest capitalists know it was built in but unspoken. They are, mostly, all the same.

While many have bought into the divide-and-conquer tactics, sold as a concept—the white supremacy—the majority of white people have not been bamboozled by the media that is owned and controlled by corporations—the new landowners.

However, the majority of white folks enjoy privileges not easily accessible to nonwhites. Some of them say they are unaware of such privileges. I say, live as a nonwhite (if it is possible) for a year, and then narrate how it felt.

Did it matter that President Barak Obama was the only president that visited a prison to show his desires for some changes? Barack knew and understood the system. It would stink if he didn't. Barack Obama knew the problems very well when, in a response to Joe the Plumber, he suggested "when you spread the wealth around, it's good for everybody."

He was responding to Samuel Joseph Wurzelbacher, popularly known as Joe the Plumber, during a stop in Ohio for the 2008 U.S. presidential campaign. That response set the conservative media on fire. It was also the rallying chant by Obama's rival, Republican nominee Senator John McCain. The senator suggested that the comment was an indication that Obama was a socialist who would engage in the redistribution of wealth.

That may bring some people to wonder whether those countries that have the PAYE tax laws understood the term—*redistribution of wealth*. If they did, what does the pay as you earn (PAYE) tax law do to wealth in those countries worldwide? What do governments do the world over with taxes?

And Republicans did whatever it took to tie his hands. Racism must be preserved. It serves capitalism well.

By the way, being a Republican does not translate to being a racist. Being a Republican does not shield Republicans from the true affairs in our society. There are poor Republicans who suffer the indignities of poverty like anyone else.

The irony of racism is that while the Republican Party championed freedoms then, they have now become a party of—no—whenever any issue clashes with the interests of the few majorly rich. They have been hijacked by the same landowners. They are now just pawns in the hands of the rich.

While some of the Democrats play good cop/bad cop and make the usual vocalization of sympathies for the downtrodden and may, from time to time, join with others to solve some token issues, they are not structurally any different from the setup of capitalism. The lots of non-white people have not changed; it's gotten worse. Check out the incarceration rate, the new slavery, if you care.

Prisoners or slaves, what are the differences?

And the few not-so-discerning among the black folks, the side line quarter-backing commentators, would, time after time, blame Barack for not doing anything or enough for black folks. Sometimes, you think they are paid by especially one particular news medium to be sarcastic.

It is unrealistic to expect a president to undo in 8 years structures that took centuries to set up. It will not take just a president, any president. It will take the whole government—the legislature, the executive, judiciary, and the country to make amendments to amend the laws that have a strangling choke hold on some of our citizens.

Even the Republicans would want to hype that sarcasm too, believing foolishly that people are quick to forget the racist plots against the real black president whose intention was to better the lots of peoples—black and white.

The system had promoted the poor white slaves. The setup system, let them buy themselves back. They let them accumulate some wealth.

The lynching of the poor white slaves was stopped while the lynching of black men increased. The poor white slaves metamorphosed into the present-day middle class. The children of the freed white slaves metamorphosed into the present-day enforcers of laws put in place by the rich landowners.

But then, because of the Thirteenth Amendment, you thought that slavery, and, therefore, racism, was over.

CHAPTER 16

The Media's Treatment of Whites vs. Nonwhites

THE MEDIA CREATES MONSTERS OUT of black people. It is in the interest of their owners. Part of the means to stay on top of the economic ladder is to sustain racism, the ingredient needed to keep American-type of capitalism going. It is part of the divide-and-conquer concept.

Now, what do you do to monsters? Apart from hating on monsters, you either avoid a monster, run from a monster, or kill a monster. The media has played, and will continue to play, a defining role in the caricature portrayal of African Americans to other Americans.

Mass media will continue to play a role in how African Americans are portrayed to white Americans. The media is attracted to bad stories. As a result, an overwhelming focus is on stories about crime, murder, violence, drugs and alcohol, gang violence, and such other antisocial behaviors among African Americans.

It is not as if such crimes and antisocial behaviors are monopolized by African Americans. It is not as if these crimes and behaviors are anything compared to the heavy criminal activities that go on in other nonblack neighborhoods.

Compared to what occurs in nonblack communities, the antisocial behaviors of a few African Americans is a slap-on-the-wrist type of behavior. That the media is guided by a distortion of facts which, in turn, they foist on the general public, is no accident.

It is by design.

How then do you make monsters out of a people if you portrayed them any better?

The media is not just the radio and TV. There are the megamedia houses in Comcast, The Walt Disney Company, 21st Century Fox, Time Warner, CBS Corporation, and Viacom. And there are others.

More damage to the black psyche was/is done by Hollywood. Just for reminders, most black films portray violent gangsterism in black lives. The type of music called rap was not promoted by Hollywood by accident.

It was designed.

And the ironic part of this whole saga is that many black folks fell for the deceit and thus, play into that trap—the stereotype of thug life. The films *Boyz in the Hood* and *Menace II Society* were multimillion-dollar success stories of criminal portrayals of young black people. I remember very well when *Boyz in the Hood* was released. There were individuals trying to relive the story line portrayed in the movie. As a result, there were fatal shootings across the United States.

This portrayal, over time, has fostered stereotypical beliefs and a perception in white America about how to view black people. It energizes the "fear" of white America about African Americans.

Recently, a movie *Straight Outta of Compton* got a lot of media hype. A few people understood right away what it means when a newspaper—*The Wrap*—had as its headline of August 13, 2015: "LA Police Beef Up Patrols Around Theaters Ahead of *Straight Outta Compton* Debut." This is a newspaper that prides itself as "covering Hollywood." The police have, a long time ago, learned to see things like the media. The caricature of the black man is working.

Have you listened to newscasters lately? You should. Start writing down a few words. As you do this, you will notice a pattern on issues involving white and black folks. There are people who have mastered how to hide the racism that must be used to keep black folks down. They have invented words to describe "bad" black behaviors. They have also mastered how to glorify the white Americans who "cannot" behave badly.

The question that must be asked is: Does it benefit the media to pander to any group in society? The answer is yes. They have no choice. The media is just a tool of the rich landowners that I keep referring to.

The media is set up to do the biddings of the rich and powerful. The media's job is to softly but methodically plant the seeds of racism, then water and nourish it so that it grows and grows. Those you see on the screens of the TV are echoing their masters' voice. They have no choice. They echo their masters so much every year, the same hours on the same days, every day.

They do it so many times, they too start to believe themselves and act accordingly. They are consciously or unconsciously promoting the divide-and-rule strategies that we talked about earlier in the beginning of this book.

In the 1980s, Michael Reich developed the Segmentation Theory or the Divide and Rule, which was an attempt to explain racism from an economic point of view. In the theory, he proposed that the ultimate goal in society is to maximize profits. As a result, the exploiters (landowners) will attempt to use any means to: (a) suppress higher wages among the exploited class, (b) weaken the bargaining power of the working class, often by attempting to split it along racial lines by promoting prejudices, (c) segregate the (poor) black community, and (d) ensure that the elite (the 1-percent landowners) benefit from the creation of stereotypes and racial prejudices against the black community.

Reich argued that the major corporations in the United States all have at least one member on each other's corporate boards of directors. Therefore, it is in the interest of these members to maximize profits while employing the above devices.

The mere fact that these corporate executives are sharing economic corporate power, combined with the sole aim of economic profit, has now created an avenue for economic discrimination. Economic discrimination is, therefore, a euphemism for capitalism.

Now the question remains: Is the media one of the tools used to promote racism? Does the elite use the media to create the needed divide and conquer in order to ensure that profits are maximized by corporations/landowners?

The mass American media is neck deep in doing the masters' bidding. They are private enterprises owned by individuals whose aim is also to maximize profits.

What if the media is government controlled? It then serves to maximize the aims of the ruling class to divide and conquer whoever is at the lower ebb of the economic ladder. It would not be discrimination in a place like Jamaica because blacks will not be singled out like they are singled out and played like a violin in the United States with the help of capitalism for the sake of capitalism.

CHAPTER 17

Affirmative Action Revisited

———

WHEN YOU REMEDY YEARS OF injustices against African Americans, it is called affirmative action. Take it a little further and some will call it socialism in America. To all who condemn affirmative action for nonwhites and women, ask them if they will exchange places with the nonwhites and women for the treatment meted out to them.

If the answer is in the affirmative, they are liars. No one—not one white male—even if crazy, would exchange the white privilege for 1 week of treatments meted out to black folks in America. If you as a white person are unwilling to accept the black treatment, it signifies that you totally understand how black folks are treated . . . *and you don't like it.*

And that brings up the question: Why are you keeping quiet? Is this the type of freedom you'd envisage in America? Why do you look the other way when part of mankind is caged to suffocate?

Discrimination has always been driven by economics. Racism and/or discrimination in America is about protecting the rich landowners using other white males as enforcers and access to wealth. The rich landowners made an easy sell to the "enforcers" by providing an array of incentives, like preferential treatment for land, jobs, loans, housing, and financing.

Blacks were initially and systemically unable to participate as enforcers of anything, thereby unable to enjoy the bounties of the capitalism. Blacks became the group on whose back capitalism was built, but who were not allowed to partake in the fruits.

Today, the rich landowners are the corporations.

Affirmative action as a concept is not new. Socialism in America is not new either. They just used a different but new name for the concept of affirmative action. When nonwhites are recipients of uplifting assistance from the government, it is described as "handouts."

When white folks receive assistance, it is said that they deservingly worked for it. It is merit. It is nation building. Like wealth, affirmative action has nothing to do with merit, talent, intelligence, or hard work.

It has everything to do with more than 400 years of being left behind. White folks had 400 years of a head start in landownership and amassing equity.

Black folks even paid taxes, which were used for assistance in building wealth . . . for white folks.

No one cried big government when the government was building wealth for white families. The government single-handedly enriched the white families using the tax money. Remember, black folks were also paying taxes and received no benefits because all government programs were designed to assist white families.

So, while black folks were paying taxes, they were barred from programs supported with their taxes. Today, some media commentators would want to make you believe that the government is giving handouts. They feign ignorance and therefore do not make mention of nonwhite taxpayers. Perhaps they were not feigning but were simply ignorant.

The noise that market forces must decide everything is simply rhetoric and hypocritical. Did market forces make available the lands and mortgage loans for white folks?

The government of the United States made it happen, not free market forces because free market forces alone cannot do that. It is time for some truth telling.

When some wish for a small government, they know exactly what they mean. When some misguided nonwhites say the same thing, you can tell they have not thought through the meaning. They bought into the "small government" argument because it was sold as being lean and mean, costing less to run.

But that is far from what small government means. When the government was subsidizing lands and housing for white folks, white folks did not call for small government then. But as soon as nonwhite folks were allowed to participate in the same government programs that assisted only white folks to accumulate wealth, all of a sudden, there is need for small government.

The call for small government is a ploy to economically stifle the poor and maintain capitalism as is.

So, what is small government?

In all practicality, small government thus translates to: Stop assisting the poor, especially nonwhites. Any attempt to assist them becomes socialism.

If you reason that affirmative action is the closest the United States government has come to acknowledging the atrocities committed against their citizens and making a token reparation-like amends, reasonable Americans cannot accuse you of telling a lie.

Good macroeconomics would make you think that if all citizens were allowed to participate in programs that would assist them to amass wealth, that there would be more people in the middle class, a bigger economy, less crimes, empty prisons, etc.

What, therefore, is the incentive to create poor people and legislate a means to keep them down? Did I hear you say capitalism? You are right. The status quo must be maintained.

Some may not see hypocrisy in this. But let us think about this rationally. If nonblacks were to empathize (for lack of a better word) with white folks, what would be a reason to discriminate against others and institutionalize racism? Let's examine a few angles.

1. Hatred? Hatred or hate is a deep emotional and extreme dislike. Such hatred can be directed against certain individuals or groups. To say hatred is the reason to keep nonwhites poor would be far-fetched. Even when nonwhites were slaves, they had cherished values of—live and let live. Disdain? Maybe, but definitely, not hatred.

2. Fear? Fear is a phobia. Phobia is the extreme aversion embedded deep in our psyches, activated when we come face-to-face with that which we fear. Some people—mostly nonblacks—are afraid of black people. Is it a fear based on facts or a belief that the black man is inherently bad, or is it a fear of repercussion emanating from what our grandfathers did to the black man? This angle is worth pursuing, but then, it is just a very lethal phobia.

3. Greed? This is more like it. Greed is good for those at the top. Greed is good for the few landowners represented by corporations now. The rich have a need to create an imaginary enemy. They do not want to be seen as the enemy, just like the corporations don't want you to know that they manage the world's resources for a select few. They hand out some minute resources, here and there, to the operators/managers of the corporations, who are the middle class. Thus, the middle class thinks they are buddy-buddy with the landowners. The landowners must provide an incentive in order to maintain a grip at their corporations, so the design is to make the middle class believe that the lower class is at that level because they are lazy and seeking handouts. Ask yourself a question. Were black people lazy

during slavery? Did black folks seek handouts during slavery? Of course, they received handouts in shapes of chitlins, pig's feet, and cow's feet. How, all of a sudden, did blacks became lazy as soon as slavery was "over"? Can you begin to see the design now?

4. By design? It is a design in plain sight. Many people cannot see it. Those who see it are incapable to do anything about it because, by design, the whole plot has been legislated into law. Just like apartheid, the various governments and departments at many levels justified the discrimination through laws that the oppressed cannot surmount. It was so then, and it is so today with little or no legislative modification in sight. Have you ever imagined why the 44th president of the United States is having so many problems with Congress? You think Congress populated by mostly old white men are giving the black president a tough time because of race?

Or . . . Do you think they hate the first black president of the Union? If you answered yes to any of these questions, you are yet to understand the workings of a country some have christened "God's own country." The fear of a black president undoing 400 years of discriminative laws, the phobia of taking down the protections of the rich landowners and the enforcers of that protection led to a section of a Congress to proclaim from day one of the black president's inauguration: "If Obama wants it, we reject it right off the bat."

This simply means an opposition to President Obama's policies on all fronts. Some were not hiding their enthusiasm for an Obama failure; they worked for it. They feared an Obama presidency that might implement programs that would invite nonwhites to participate, thus engaging in capitalism. New slogans like "Take our country back" were dusted up for reuse.

It was strategic.

They were all noises meant to drown some of Obama's signature programs like the affordable care act, popularly known as Obamacare.

It has always been by design. And some are willing to keep it that way forever.

The government of the United States has been helping and assisting the populace for hundreds of years. The problem was that nonwhites were not allowed to participate. It is the same today, like it was yesterday, with or without cosmetic legislation.

Whites have been receiving affirmative action for the past 400 years. They just called it different names. It was racial preference.

They never saw it as racial preference or privilege until laws were passed to remedy years of legislated racial discrimination. All of a sudden, the government was accused of tampering with market forces.

When the government helps white folks, it is called nation building—a good macroeconomic policy, but when same government helps nonwhites, it is described as a handout, or better still, affirmative action.

While some are clamoring to make affirmative action illegal by advancing reasons, the same reasons that indirectly exposes the same greed and discrimination that existed then to justify their stand, they purposefully turn blind eyes to the reasons why affirmative action laws were really enacted in the first place.

When some folks say that affirmative action discriminates against them, one can at least fathom some reasons they think so. However, what is the excuse for some nonwhites agreeing with opponents of affirmative action?

The truth of the matter is not that sons and daughters of white slaves metamorphosed into the middle class they are today because they worked harder or because they are smarter. To believe that is the height of tomfoolery. The truth is socialism—a word we pretend to hate today was the reason some of us are middle class.

Let us dissect the growth to the middle class using a set of programs operated by the United States government.

What is the Federal Housing Administration (FHA)? (From the FHA Web site)

The Federal Housing Administration, generally known as "FHA," provides mortgage insurance on loans made by FHA-approved lenders throughout the United States and its territories. FHA insures mortgages on single-family and multifamily homes, including manufactured homes and hospitals. It is the largest insurer of mortgages in the world, insuring over 34 million properties since its inception in 1934.

What is FHA Mortgage Insurance?

FHA mortgage insurance provides lenders with protection against losses as the result of homeowners defaulting on their mortgage loans. The lenders bear less risk because FHA will pay a claim to the lender in the event of a homeowner's default. Loans must meet certain requirements established by FHA to qualify for insurance.

Prior to the establishment of the FHA, no bank was willing to give loans to a mass of people—not even white men. No bank was willing to take that risk. So, Americans were stuck in neutral when it came to borrowing for housing.

This is government's intervention in the economy in order to assist folks in creating wealth. You are probably used to people shouting at the top of their lungs about why the government must not interfere in the economy. Well, you can see that government intervention led to the creation of wealth because people (white) were able to buy houses and start building and amassing huge wealth from way back. Most nonwhites are still expecting a better life in "heaven"—an afterlife.

The question one may be tempted to ask now is: When is it OK for a big or small government?

Another question could be: Is small government better than a big government?

The answers to the above questions could be obvious, but then it can be colored by race. If a government program is legislated to benefit and give a head start to only white folks, it is a good program. No questions asked or complaints raised.

However, if such a program allowed an all-race participation, you start hearing the government-is-too-big argument. All excuses are then laid on the table about why it is a bad program and too big.

Can you think of a program that is facing condemnation lately? The one where some people have vowed to repeal? Can you now see the reason why they feel it must be repealed? Can you also think of other programs that benefit farmers but have not drawn any campaign for repeal?

Can you see why?

The real marrow in the bone is its ability to serve the function of providing red and white blood cells to the body. The body knows when it needs more or less of the blood cells. The economy therefore under watchful eyes can be manipulated with a good intention of creating wealth and/or making a better living for all. Governments all over the world have also learned the art of expanding or contracting an economy with either starting a new program or modifying existing ones.

So, when you hear people shouting that small government is better than big government, try to understand where the opinion is coming from. A big government—a government that creates programs to assist in creating wealth for all and thereby expanding the economy when the time is right is not necessarily an expensive and inefficient way to accomplish policies and goals.

Neither does a small government mean prudency, cost-effectiveness, efficiency, or better. If anything, small government is beginning to mean a term used for depriving some people a means to wealth.

It has become a term connoting, derogatively, that big government is inefficient. What opponents of big governments won't tell you is that they worry that every other person will be allowed to participate in government programs which, ultimately, assist in building wealth for all. American-like capitalism, if you did not forget, is nothing but racism.

Programs which were exclusively a head start for white folks for years had become exclusive to nonwhites after passing a few civil right laws here and there. This does not eliminate the head start advantage. Prior to programs such as the FHA, there was a program popularly known as the headrights.

> As per Wikipedia, *"a headright is a legal grant of land to settlers. Headrights are most notable for their role in the expansion of the thirteen British colonies in North America; the Virginia Company of London gave headrights to settlers, and the Plymouth Company followed suit. The headright system was used in several colonies, including Maryland, Georgia, North Carolina, and South Carolina. Most headrights were for 1 to 1,000 acres (4.0 km²) of land, and were given to anyone willing to cross the Atlantic Ocean and help populate the colonies. Headrights were granted to anyone who would pay for the transportation costs of a laborer or indentured servant. These land grants consisted of*

50 acres (200,000 m²) for someone newly moving to the area and 100 acres (0.40 km²) for people previously living in the area. By giving the land to the landowning masters, the indentured servants had little or no chance to procure their own land. This kept many colonials poor and led to strife between the poor servants and wealthy landowners."

There were programs where the government took the responsibility to shoulder the risks that would emanate from huge financial undertakings with regards to insuring house loans through the FHA.

While the government chose to shoulder the risks, the banks simply restricted participation by race. Thus, only one race could use the program to attain wealth.

This, however, is not the point.

The point is that the government provided a social service and no one seemed to be shouting then. There was no mouthing off that it was a housing affirmative action for white folks. So, while the white race has been benefitting from the government since 1934, other nonwhites have been systematically barred, and it is all A-OK.

This has always been the modus operandi in all other facets of American life—racist capitalism, otherwise referred to as entrepreneurial capitalism.

Have you noticed arguments by some academics on how affirmative action is a bad thing? Have you heard some nonwhite folks join white folks in the condemnation of affirmative action? Some argue about all the bad side of the program. According to some of them, there is nothing good in affirmative action.

Nonwhite people who join white folks in highlighting the dumbing down of education or such other areas do so because they want to equate the black man's intelligence with the white man's. They, perhaps, do not want a dumbing down of their qualifications. Perhaps they needed a white man's certification. Such thought patterns are silly.

To such people, I say: Be confident in your blackness. Be confident in your qualifications. That you made it thus far is an affirmation that you are a survivor no matter the circumstances. Keep your head up!

It will be nice if we understood why there is so much campaigning against anything dealing with affirmative action.

Are those who are antiaffirmative action also anti-FHA loans? What kind of assistance do they think such loans were/ are for?

Sometimes, one wishes that the future of affirmative action is brighter than light. Affirmative action is yet to manifest in all facets of American life. How much of affirmative action is in the police, the courts, the universities, housing, jobs, etc.?

If there is anywhere affirmative action is well pronounced, it is in the prison population.

How many of the antiaffirmative loudmouths have you heard complaining about why the jails are more affirmative than the rest of America?

Did you know it is cheaper to have affirmative action in the classrooms of the universities and technical schools than in the prisons? Why is America willing to pay more to incarcerate— especially the nonwhites—than to train them?

CHAPTER 18

Your Food Market

―――

YOU MAY BEGIN TO WONDER why and what foods have to do with your freedoms. A lot. If the system is willing to incarcerate a people for any cause—or no cause—what else do you think the system would not do?

If a system is willing to test killer diseases on black people, what other bad things do you think the system won't be used for? You think the system is fair?

Do you think that when drugs/medicines are researched for white folks, they use nonwhites for the research? The system is set up the way it is, in all things . . . foods included.

Here are some sources of food available in heavily populated inner cities.

1. All the fast-food joints

and

2. All the liquor stores on every other block.

All the fast-food joints and others are located approximately a mile apart for easy and maximum access. They provide easy access and fast service for substandard foods that would guarantee you a hospital bed soon in the future.

Apart from the aforementioned abodes where many people get breakfast, lunch, and dinner, you have places like Key Food, AP, and your nearest local grocery stores where you walk a block or two to get your groceries.

For one, the food in the local grocery is mostly expensive. It is mostly inorganic quality and expensive, and some of the shoppers are mostly unaware. Even where the shoppers are aware, there are hardly any choices. If they did have choices, perhaps they would know they were buying mostly genetically modified foods.

Of all the fast foods, you will notice less Dunkin' Donuts and Starbucks in these neighborhoods. More people are exposed to alcohol than to coffee. That coffee shops are breaking through to these neighborhoods today is, perhaps, good news.

Meanwhile, you drive some miles—30–45 miles—out of the inner city, and you find stores like Sam's, Walmart, BJ's, with car parking facilities, where you shop in convenience. A convenience that is not usually associated with locations in urban areas.

That is not even the lure or the point.

In places like Sam's, you buy in quantity and in quality, and cheap. And you are happy that you find this new place. Could you take it one step further and ask why the Sam's and BJ's, etc., are not in your neighborhoods?

Do you ever wonder why the word "kosher" is associated with quality and nature? Take it a litter further, Muslims have the "halal" quality standards. While some prescribe organic foods, kosher, or halal quality standards, the foods in some urban grocery stores are simply genetically modified products that are deemed fit for shoppers who pay with "checks" received from government programs.

If, as a shopper, you pay close attention and/or do some research just by observing stores in various locations, you will quickly notice that mostly black neighborhoods face double jeopardy when it comes to good supermarkets' access . . .supermarkets, where the shelves are stocked with fresh, organic quality and cheap products. There is also a choice of fresh produce—organic or inorganic.

After shopping in places like Sam's as compared to the local grocer in your locale, you can calculate your losses and come to the conclusion that it is, indeed, expensive to be poor and very cheap to be rich. Not only does your wallet suffer a hiccup, the available inorganic foods slowly do the body harm over time. We live in a today where consumers are supposed to vote with their wallets. The consumers, even if they realize the differences between organic and inorganic foods, do not have the power to evoke change by voting with the most important tool at their disposal . . . their wallets.

Their wallets are likely to contain food stamps. Today, it is a well-known fact that if you want a cleaner environment and healthier food, you choose organic products. It's a double whammy for poor people.

Initially, many people, especially immigrants, do not notice this. They are happy for what they consider to be food aplenty. To the experienced and healthy conscious shopper, lack of quality supermarket access for mostly minority neighborhoods is not news.

Economists and activists have been loud in saying that poor, minority neighborhoods have no access to supermarkets with fresh organic quality produce in large quantities and cheaper prices. Cheaper means the same as what is available in nonwhite neighborhoods.

Quality is the watchword here because in the inner cities, it's mostly GMOs (genetically modified organisms)—you are only accelerating the speed to acquiring those ailments associated with GMOs. Products available in minority locales are not the healthiest of foods. Some of these foods would slowly but surely kill you. You should search why the diabetic rate is so high in such neighborhoods.

Now, you know at least one of the reasons.

That which could not be attained by arrests and imprisonment could easily be achieved through the foods you have access to. You get lower prices and high quality products shopping in stores like Sam's, BJ's, and Walmart. When a comparison is made of Sam's and the local grocery stores, the benefits are as clear as day and night. Almost always, supermarket access in sections of urban areas is not tied to quality of products; it is tied solely to profits.

And this begs the question: Why are Walmart and other wholesalers not found in black neighborhoods? The excuse is there are difficulties acquiring the necessary city permits. Another excuse is that the mom-and-pop outlets are against such big stores because they fear being put out of business.

Do you buy into that argument? It's an argument that wants to convince that it is better to pay high price for low-quality food products.

There is no easy answer. There is the environmental, political, as well as economic reasons.

Ask a few of your friends or coworkers how many miles they drive to get to the nearest supermarket. You may be able to tell what kind of neighborhood they live in and the quality of life they enjoy by the number of miles it takes to reach the nearest supermarket.

While there is a finding that it takes approximately 1.8 miles to the nearest large grocery or supermarket, it may take some people of color nearly *60 miles* to get to a supermarket that is associated with quality products and money-saving advantages.

Let's take a look at studies from ERS. The Economic Research Service (ERS) is a component of the United States Department of Agriculture and a principal agency of the Federal Statistical System of the United States.

ERS is a primary source of economic research and analysis providing timely information on economic and policy issues related to agriculture, food, the environment, and rural America.

Here are some of their findings:

Access to a supermarket or large grocery store is a problem for a small percentage of households. Results indicate that some consumers are constrained in their ability to access affordable nutritious food because they live far from a supermarket or large grocery store and do not have easy access to transportation. Three pieces of evidence corroborate this conclusion:

- *Of all U.S. households, 2.3 million, or 2.2 percent, live more than a mile from a supermarket and do not have access to a vehicle. An additional 3.4 million households, or 3.2 percent of all households, live between one-half to 1 mile and do not have access to a vehicle.*

- *Area-based measures of access show that 23.5 million people live in low-income areas (areas where more than 40 percent of the population have income at or below 200 percent of federal poverty thresholds) that are more than 1 mile from a supermarket or large grocery store. However, not all of these 23.5 million people have low income. If estimates are restricted to consider only low-income people in low-income areas, then 11.5 million people, or 4.1 percent of the total U.S. population, live in low-income areas more than 1 mile from a supermarket.*

- *Data on time use and travel mode show that people living in low-income areas with limited access spend significantly more time (19.5 minutes) traveling to a grocery store than the national average (15 minutes). However, 93 percent of*

*those who live in low-income areas with limited access trav-
eled to the grocery store in a vehicle they or another household member drove.*

*These distance- and time-based measures are national estimates
that do not consider differences between rural and urban areas in
terms of distance, travel patterns, and retail market coverage. Urban
core areas with limited food access are characterized by higher levels
of racial segregation and greater income inequality. In small-town
and rural areas with limited food access, the lack of transportation
infrastructure is the most defining characteristic.*

*These areas or distance-based results are in line with a nation-
ally representative survey of U.S. households conducted in 2001.
Responses to direct questions about food access show that nearly 6
percent of all U.S. households did not always have the food they
wanted or needed because of access-related problems. More than
half of these households also lacked enough money for food. It is
unclear whether food access or income constraints were relatively
greater barriers for these households.*

Perhaps the part of the report to pay close attention to is this:

*Supermarkets and large grocery stores have lower prices than smaller
stores. A key concern for people who live in areas with limited access is that they rely on small grocery or convenience stores that may
not carry all the foods needed for a healthy diet and that may offer
these foods and other food at higher prices. This report examines
whether prices of similar foods vary across retail outlet types and
whether the prices actually paid by consumers vary across income
levels. These analyses use proprietary household-level data that contain information on food items purchased by approximately 40,000*

demographically representative households across the United States. Results from these analyses show that when consumers shop at convenience stores, prices paid for similar goods are, on average, higher than at supermarkets.

Therefore, your pockets are depleted and your health, slowly but steadily, takes a beating.

Another article published in the not-so-distant past, narrates how "some researchers from Johns Hopkins University wanted to see how different neighborhood traits—poverty and racial makeup—were related to the problem."

For instance, what did it mean to be in a poorer white neighborhood versus a wealthier black neighborhood?

The researchers from Johns Hopkins stated: . . . *compared access to supermarkets, smaller grocery stores, and convenience stores in largely black, Latino, white, and racially integrated neighborhoods in a national sample of more than 65,000 census tracts. Earlier research showed that convenience stores and groceries, which are smaller than supermarkets, stock foods higher in fat, sugar, and salt.*

The study found that living in a poor, mostly black neighborhood presented "a double disadvantage" in supermarket access. Unsurprisingly, poor black neighborhoods had fewer supermarkets than wealthier black neighborhoods.

But they also had fewer supermarkets than poor white neighborhoods, suggesting that race still played a role apart from poverty. In fact, the study showed that black neighborhoods with little poverty had fewer supermarkets, on average, than high-poverty white areas.

The study found that it's not simply an issue of poverty; in fact, a racially segregated poor black neighborhood is at an additional disadvantage simply because it is predominantly black.

Researchers wrote that the supermarket shortage appeared to be more severe in urban, poor black neighborhoods than rural ones, suggesting that strategies to improve access to healthy food should not be rolled out nationwide, but targeted at disadvantaged urban areas.

"The patterns were somewhat different for Latino neighborhoods: Though they had fewer supermarkets than white neighborhoods, Latino areas had more grocery stores, no matter their poverty level" Bower said that other studies suggest groceries in Latino areas may sell healthier food than those in black neighborhoods, which means their health effects might be different.

The study also found that white neighborhoods generally had the most convenience stores, and black neighborhoods the fewest. However, if white neighborhoods "have equally good access to supermarkets and high-quality foods, they may not be as reliant on the convenience stores as a regular source of food," Bower wrote.

The Johns Hopkins study used race and poverty data from the 2000 census, overlaid with information about supermarkets and other stores from the commercial database InfoUSA.

The bigger question should be—Why this is so? Why are the big supermarkets located far away from the minority locales? An attempt to answer this question will ultimately lead you to all the other systemic practices in places designed to cage the poor and nonwhites.

Studies after studies in different aspects of life for the nonwhites is nothing near that of white folks in the quality-of-life area.

The practices to box in nonwhites is so systemic in every aspect, it includes food. The inorganic foods end up in small grocery stores located in poor neighborhoods. Some end up in nonwhite neighborhoods occupied by poor peoples.

And if you are still wondering and doubting—wait until water is discussed.

CHAPTER 19

Your Water Quality

You may immediately start to wonder why anyone would tie water to racism and discrimination and capitalism. You may even think that this is an overkill. This book was already in the works before the Flint, Michigan, water crises. Flint, Michigan, serves as a mirror into other black and poor neighborhoods. Adjustments had to be made to accommodate the Flint water crisis.

You may think it is an overkill. No, it is not an overkill. It is just the way it is. Flint garnered world attention because they would not fix the problem fast enough like they take care of problems in rich enclaves.

If they did, no one would be talking about Flint, Michigan. The poor neighborhoods without such media attention like Flint, Michigan, are dying slowly.

We learned from history where a source of water was poisoned. It was a war tactic. When there is discrimination in every facet of the American life, the delay in fixing Flint's water crisis became a new low. Where the officials should have directed their energies to fixing the problem, they resorted to killing time by blaming one another while people are getting sick and sicker.

Whether the Flint, Michigan, water crisis was allowed to happen intentionally or as a result of negligence is arguable. What is not arguable is the negligence that followed after the problem was known. Rather than deal with the problem head-on, officers responsible for solving the crisis started foot dragging and buck passing. Now, you start wondering why there was so much foot dragging.

When a people are discriminated against, mishaps such as the Flint, Michigan, water crisis become a source for various conspiracies. After all, it was a crisis in a majority black enclave. The truth of the matter is: There were other mishaps we can draw examples from. You are welcome to draw your own conclusions.

When nonwhite neighborhoods were experiencing the scourge of drugs in the 1980s and 1990s, the attitude of the authorities was that of "it's them; it's their problem."

Is it therefore any surprise that the same lackluster attitude was experienced and exposed again in Flint, Michigan? If this crisis was affecting a majority white community, the authorities would have responded swiftly to the initial reports. As you may be aware, authorities are now responding swiftly to drug crisis now ravaging white neighborhoods. For those with drug problems, treatment is the chosen option. Previously, black people with drug problems did not get treatment. They got incarcerated.

Contaminated water is no different. It is a crisis.

Tainted water can make consumers stupid and ultimately kill them. It is the job of the authorities to provide clean water. It is the function of every city, state, and the EPA to provide the useful tools for examining drinking water quality in every major metropolitan statistical area of the United States. This was a serious indictment of the EPA. There was a failure at all levels.

The tool should encompass all drinking water providers serving all of the United States. Although most cities and states meet this requirement according to data available, contaminant concentrations between metropolitan statistical areas vary significantly though drinking waters, within these areas, have generally met the U.S. EPA's Safe Drinking Water standards.

Now, that is the expectation.

You have heard about the water contamination in Flint, Michigan. You may have also heard of contamination in Sebring, Ohio. It was reported in the news that the Ohio Environmental Protection Agency knew in August 2015 that there was lead leakage into the water system of Sebring, Ohio.

State representatives called on the director of the Ohio EPA to publicly answer questions regarding evidence of lead exposure in the northeast Ohio village.

The problems were not isolated to those two areas. In Houston County, Alabama, 58 percent of tested children showed signs of lead in their blood. In nine other counties where tests were done, the federal government was told that the tested individuals were showing 10 percent of lead poisoning tests as positive.

In 2014, approximately 50 percent of all the counties nationwide did not even bother to report their test data. What this means is that more people, especially children, could be in danger and not know it.

They could suffer lead poisoning and thus, irreversible brain damage. Some possible complications could be behavior or attention problems, slowed body growth, reduced IQ, kidney damage, hearing problems, and repeated failures at school. Can you imagine being afflicted with some or all of the above complications?

If you are nonwhite, you are most likely to suffer these complications. Chances are, the infrastructures in your neighborhoods are old and rusted and seeping lead into the water like in Flint, Michigan, and you have no priority in getting the infrastructures fixed.

That is the truth. If you don't understand that, there is so much you do not understand about your freedoms.

Racism has one truth if truth is not bent.

Statistics have it that lead poisoning is more than twice likely to affect black children than white children.

The real question is: Why do those in charge of our waters pull our legs when crises arise in poor communities? Communities most likely to suffer lead poisoning are in poor neighborhoods. Such communities are subject to the long-lasting problems of lead.

Other neighborhoods suffer seeping lead issues. The difference is that the problems are fixed promptly. There is little chance that the people in these other neighborhoods are allowed to suffer brain damages caused by lead.

It is not as if the problems are insurmountable. Such problems were surmountable when they happened in some zip codes. If the problem happens in the not-so-rich zip codes, the solution to the problem becomes complicated, as you can glean from the Flint, Michigan, example. It is suggestive from the Flint example that these problems are solved faster . . . or slower . . . depending on your zip code.

If you are consuming tainted water in your zip code, what are the chances that the prison water is tested and tested often? Some of these prisons are old, and so are the pipes that carry water to them. As you may have already known, nonwhites make up the better population of the private and federal prisons. If the "free" in the neighborhoods are not cared for, you think the incarcerated would be cared for?

If you are carted away to jail for the littlest of excuses to fill some prisons somewhere because your existence means little or nothing to those who are instituting these systemic discriminating rules, why would you assume that such authorities will be quick in changing and/or replacing rusty pipes in your neighborhoods? By the way, who is your mayor, police chief, or local attorney general? How many times have you written to or called their offices with a complaint or compliment?

Those that made laws to dehumanize, kill, reduce your population, reduce your ability to think and learn, can equally achieve the same results by letting you choke on contaminated water. There are, after all, many ways to skin a cat, like the old saying goes.

Pipes get old. They rust. We all know that. The racism and discrimination come when some infrastructures in some zip codes are given priority maintenance over zip codes predominantly occupied by the poor and nonwhites.

Simply put, if your life means nothing to those in charge, how can they see what is wrong with your water—contaminated or not?

Racism is indeed a disease. It is manifested in various ways. Sometimes, it does not manifest at all, and that is the worst type. It must be treated. For example, if the majority of the death penalty victims were white folks, the death penalty in the United States would have been banned eons ago. The application of the U.S. death penalty is known to be unfair, arbitrary, and racially biased. In fact, whether a defendant receives a death sentence is dependent, not on the merits of the case as much as on his or her skin color—and the race of the victim—and perhaps the county in which the murder case was pursued and prosecuted.

No matter how you argue it, race and capital punishment in the United States have always been inseparable. Race is the face of freedoms. Statistically looking at the representation of black and other nonwhite prisoners on death row, it is hardly surprising that of the nearly 150 convicts convicted of capital offenses that were found innocent since 1973, approximately 65 percent have been of people of color.

The system was already making life for nonwhites difficult. Contaminated water is the icing on the cake. The water crisis is perhaps no crisis. After all, it makes the job of limiting the poor easier.

It was never this bad, even in former Southern Rhodesia or apartheid South Africa.

CHAPTER 20

Housing & Infrastructure

———

DISCRIMINATION IS ENDEMIC IN THIS sector of the economy. Those who live it see it. The planners of the system made sure that in everything, nonwhites are discriminated against. In everything that makes life worth living, apartheid was inserted to make life miserable for people of color.

Even the infrastructures were built to segregate and discriminate. While segregation can provide certain protective benefits for nonwhites living among their own racial groups, it becomes problematic if accompanied by persistent, overlapping inequalities.

Housing discrimination has always been a pervasive problem in the United States. It is also severely underreported. The federal government recognizes this pervasive problem; hence, a law was enacted to give voice to the voiceless.

The U.S. Department of Housing and Urban Development (HUD) estimates over 2 million instances of housing discrimination occur every year, but fewer than 1 percent is reported. Perhaps people are not reporting it because like in other spheres, many people are unaware that they have been victims of housing discrimination. It is so subtle that people do not even give a thought to it.

Let us say that there are two people—one white, the other black—with the same job, salary, and credit rating. It is a given that one will get the lower rate for loans. The nonwhite borrower is likely to get a higher interest loan. In the final analysis, one will pay back $500,000 and the other $300,000 for the same quality house in separate but unequal neighborhoods.

You may argue that the creation of the Federal Housing Administration (FHA) to insure lenders against the risk of default on mortgages fundamentally transformed what it meant to own a house in America. It was an attempt to promote home ownership for all peoples.

In spite of the risk involved, the FHA decided to insure low-down-payment, long-term mortgages in an attempt to promote homeownership. In order to achieve that goal, the FHA needed to change dozens of federal and state laws to make those mortgages legal.

The FHA had a very good argument for doing it this way because they understood that the increased rate of default on such loans would not threaten lenders' safety and soundness.

However, a closer look at these policies, which are logical and benign on the surface, had, in the long term, produced devastating results for nonwhites and poor Americans. The FHA's core insurance program, section 203(b), systematically discriminates against African Americans.

And this is how: The FHA underwriting guidelines is based on an economically and historically flawed understanding of a change—the change of neighborhoods from white homeowners to nonwhite homeowners where home values are estimated based on neighborhoods where the same houses in white neighborhoods are valued more than the same houses in nonwhite neighborhoods.

The same guidelines were to rate a neighborhood's suitability for insurance based on racial composition. Thus, such guidelines encouraged and even mandated racial conditions for insurance, thereby discouraging integrated neighborhoods.

Bottom line is that the FHA produced guidelines that systemically puts money in the pockets of white homeowners while shortchanging people of color by the use of two valuation techniques for the same houses—one for white folks, the other for nonwhites.

It is OK to be reminded that prior to the New Deal reforms, home-ownership was primarily for reasons of consumption—not necessarily for investment. But through the New Deal reforms, homeownership became the primary mechanism that most Americans, the middle class, that is, used and continue to use it to amass assets.

Presently, over 59 percent of the total assets of middle-class Americans are held in owner-occupied homes. Thus, the real question is: How much of such assets are in the hands of nonwhites? That is the question. And therein lies all the years of accumulated segregation and discrimination.

CHAPTER 21

I Can Do Cannabis, You Cannot

WHEN CRACK COCAINE AND DRUGS like it were ravaging the nonwhite neighborhoods, the authorities saw an opportunity. It was the opportunity to kill more birds with one stone, so to speak. Before this, to keep the blacks down was through unemployment, no motivation to go to school, arrests and lockup, bad foods, long sentences for minor offenses, the death penalty, etc.

The crack epidemic was an opportunity to flood the black neighborhoods with police in order to arrest crack traders and buyers, addicts and kingpins, and murderers, all mostly nonwhites. It was an opportunity to haul all of them to jails. People were making billions of dollars out of the misery of mostly nonwhites.

Did you know that a company—Corrections Corporation of America—the largest for-profit prison company in America, spends over $1 million annually to fight against the legalization of cannabis— the plant popularly known as Indian hemp, or simply, weed?

Do you care to think of one reason why the company would want to do that?

The simple reason is this: Any changes in the law with respect to drugs and other controlled substances like cannabis would affect the quantity of persons arrested, convicted, and jailed, thereby reducing or potentially eliminating the demand for the services and facilities of Corrections Corporation of America.

Remember that nonwhites are six times more likely to be arrested than white folks. So, the bottom line is that some people are reaping billions by benefitting from the mass incarceration of mostly poor and nonwhite people. Is it not interesting that people are buying stocks to profit from Corrections Corporation of America? It was like ancient America. It is like trading on African American men all over again.

Do you think it is important to find out if your senator or representative benefit from donations coming from Corrections Corporation of America?

Corrections Corporation of America is America's leading provider of public-private partnership corrections solutions. They claim to serve state, local, and the federal governments.

Corrections Corp. of America trades at the New York Stock Exchange. Its stock was trading at $32.20 at the time of writing this book. Its 52-week high was $40.89. The company has a market capitalization of $3.77 billion. From a page on the Web, we read: *"Corrections Corporation of America is a company that owns and manages private prisons and detention centers and operates others on a concession basis. Co-founded by Thomas W. Beasley, a leader in the Republican Party, Doctor Robert Crants, and T. Don Hutto in 1983, it received initial investments from Hospital Corporation of America's founder Jack C. Massey, the Tennessee Valley Authority, and Vanderbilt University."*

African Americans, and by extension, Americans, do not travel far and wide unless for pleasure. And that is done by well-to-do Americans. Rich nonwhites are far in between when it comes to traveling around the world.

So, who are the Americans connected with the drug trade in black neighborhoods? If you do a little research, you will not be disappointed at the results. Sometimes, you have to be smart to ask the right questions, and you find that the answers are right there in plain sight.

You may now start to wonder how the drugs infiltrated and saturated the so-called ghettos. Have you wondered about that? If I was planning a decrease to groups of people I detest, a very good way to do it is to introduce drugs such as heroin, cocaine, and others into that community.

Once that is successful, I sit back and watch that community self-destruct. We can as well introduce any other killer disease(s). We can accomplish these goals, and much more, just like that. It is that easy.

You may argue that peoples of various ethnicities worldwide do drugs. You may also argue that peoples of various class levels do drugs. Yes, that is true. The difference is that no police officers are standing in front of their doors waiting with handcuffs to haul them to jails. In fact, this is how it was handled in nonwhite neighborhoods where the norm is overpolicing.

When this scourge was ravaging the black communities, the attitude of policy makers was: *It's them.* So, they looked the other way. It was time to look for solutions—good solutions, but policy makers simply let them burn. They, however, provided some bad solutions. They incarcerated young black men, and sometimes, it was a prison term for life. The unlucky ones died or were killed.

Now that the scourge has escaped the boundaries of the ghetto to white America, the attitude of the policy makers has changed. They finally saw drug addiction for what it is—an affliction, a disease.

Why do you think that is so?

All America is now suffering the drug scourge. Children of policy makers are now victims. The genie has escaped the bottle. It is no longer the ghetto's genie. Now, it is America's problem. It is no longer the problem of the people, authorities and the media love to paint as monsters.

The point here is: Put a mirror in policy-makers faces so that they can see the double standards. You are supposed to get an interest in who and be outraged over those conglomerates—public or private—that had ties to drug trafficking.

The 1980s crack cocaine epidemic devastated black neighborhoods, destroyed black families, and put thousands of young black men in prison. If it was a plan, nothing beats that because it was a massive success.

Since I started taking an interest in the population of black people in America, the percentage proportion to America's population has remained the same—no movement. There have been movements in the population of others, however.

If there was a plan to keep the black population contained, through any window of opportunity (created or not), it is working. Never forget that once arrested for drug offences, that arrestee's ability to participate in ordinary activities such as employment is greatly affected.

It is a double standard rooted in racist capitalism. It is okay to keep a blind eye when it is a "black problem" so that ultimately, the population of the "monsters" would be reduced. Now that policy makers are recognizing that drug addiction is a disease, it produces a couple of things:

1. Treatment for drug users
2. No arrest, no jail time
3. No lifetime in jail
4. No killings by officers of the law

Can you imagine the opposite of numbers 1 through 4? The opposite was what nonwhite peoples suffered and endured.

Meanwhile, somewhere in Colorado, something happened. Cannabis plant made history again. Hemp became the intended, or unintended, victim of the United States' prohibition on cannabis —it fell into the Marijuana Tax Act of 1937 and is presently blacklisted by the DEA under the Controlled Substances Act. The plant is about to make millionaires out of Colorado natives. It's beginning to be seen by many as the solution to any number of illnesses, and many states are making provisions for medical marijuana laws.

It is the plant classified as a drug. There have been numerous proposals in the United States to remove this plant from Schedule I of the Controlled Substances Act.

Many people have been hauled to jail for buying and smoking pot. Families have been destroyed for possessing a small quantity of this drug. The largest group at the receiving end of this devastation are the nonwhite families.

White neighborhoods have largely been insulated from such devastation. Sometimes, white students in colleges even experiment with marijuana without the slightest concern for prosecution.

While black and brown communities are overpoliced and penalized at unprecedented rates, the wealthier white communities remain largely insulated. Now, legal marijuana is the fastest-growing new business in the U.S. You would think that those who suffered the indignities and devastations caused by illegal marijuana would be 50 percent the beneficiaries of fortunes made available by legal marijuana.

Colorado, the first state to allow retail recreational marijuana sales to adults, age 21 and older, has projected nearly a billion dollars in combined wholesale and retail marijuana sales annually. This is not an aggressive forecast. Marijuana was legalized in Colorado in 2012.

The irony of it all is that very few nonwhites can benefit from this. It is estimated that the legal pot market could hit $20 billion annually by the year 2020.

At one point, there were 1,200 dispensaries where you could get legal marijuana in Colorado. Of the 1,200 dispensaries, only *one* belonged to a person of color. The same system and people that criminalized and penalized millions of people of color for $10 worth of marijuana will now benefit with an almost 100 percent of white folks with dispensaries.

They, therefore, make all the billions, and people of color are, once again, left on the wayside. Meanwhile, black and brown people in most other states are still being incarcerated over marijuana, while white folks in Colorado are standing to make billions of dollars.

Do you now see and understand how your zip code determines your level of freedom? Do you see how your zip code determines a great deal of your ability to live a quality life? The zip code determines your mortgage, your insurance rate, education, medical care, how you are policed, how much you are over- or underpoliced, or not policed at all. Your zip code determines who can open carry a gun.

The real reason why black and brown peoples cannot share in the windfall bounty from marijuana in Colorado is the entrenched systemic racism. Before the law took effect, the records of most of the young able-bodied black and brown people within that population had been tainted by arrests and prison terms.

Once you have a felony, you are barred from the marijuana trade. Now, they cannot work or get loans to start businesses. They need clean records to get licenses. They cannot participate because their hands have been soiled by a system that set them up for failure. It is systemic.

If, at this juncture, you are screaming "racism," you still do not get the whole picture yet. Somebody could be racist, but they should not be allowed to have power over you. The system is set up with laws that power disproportionately an enforcement that favors favoritism and segregation. This is the reason racism has teeth. The racist-backed laws are the reason why they systemically have power over the targeted group. That is the setup. Nonwhites cannot get any respite until they hold the feet of their local and national leaders—Republican or Democratic—accountable. It will be very difficult to get these systemic laws changed without holding your representatives accountable.

CHAPTER 22

If Health Is Wealth

THE WAY MOST MINORITIES EXPERIENCED it . . .

An African proverb says: *Health is wealth.* If health is wealth, then not all people in the United States are allowed to participate in wealth. Our capitalist experiences must have made that abundantly clear. Health as wealth is not only significant to you, but it also affects the availability of choices. Like your finances, you make healthcare decisions regarding choices throughout your life's activities. Therefore, your health status is an important ingredient in your social position, today, and for your future well-being.

But not everybody has had the opportunity to experience the healthcare benefits in the United States simply because it is wealth. As in wealth, some people want to keep access for poor people to the barest minimum.

Have you met some animal lovers who really take care of their pets? When the pets get sick, it is as if the owner is sick. The pet is quickly rushed to a vet to be treated. Most times, the owners never wait for their pets to get sick. They adhere to a periodical medical checkup. They choose preventive health care for their animals.

The same is said of slave owners in the days of yore. A sick slave was an unproductive slave. Slave owners made sure that their slaves were fit and ready to go. Did the slaves have better medical attention then than some poor folks are getting now?

If you are born poor, with limited or no opportunities for quality education, and the burden of racism is bearing down on you, all you have left as your wealth is health. Lose that too and you are gone. Can you envision just one way your health can be taken away from you? Have you had the privilege of a personal doctor? Can you compare their services to the general practice in public hospitals?

Understanding the nature of the healthcare system operations is critical to appreciating the racist nature of healthcare institutions.

If the unspoken plan is to eliminate or limit a group—any group—would your plan include but not be limited to . . .

1. Provision of the finest medicines available?
2. Provision of the best available medical technologies in your community hospitals?
3. Provision of a conducive environment for childbearing and child-rearing?

Despite significant advances in the diagnosis and treatment of most chronic diseases, there is no denying that ethnic minorities tend to receive a lower quality of medical care than the nonminority, and that patients of minority ethnicities experience greater morbidity and mortality from various chronic diseases than white folks do in the United States.

That has always been the pattern. A look at a few reports will confirm this. Hardly is research for new drugs done using people of color . . . except as guinea pigs. When there was the need to test the efficacy of a new drug to cure syphilis, nonwhites served as the guinea pigs. Do not be quick to forget the notorious Tuskegee Experiment.

The Tuskegee syphilis experimentation was an infamous clinical study conducted up to 1972 by the U.S. Public Health Service. They used people of color to study the natural progression of untreated syphilis in black men in Alabama under the disguise of receiving free health care from the United States government.

Do not be deceived. The more things seem to change, the more they remain the same. The recent Ebola outbreak in West Africa is very interesting in this regard. The point being that if it can happen in the United States in our not-so-distant past, worse things are happening elsewhere.

Another good example is in the area of vitamin D. The book *Sunshine Vitamin & Black People* came to a conclusion that black folks are beginning to suffer from diseases associated with vitamin D deficiency today. The book suggests that because not enough studies have been done using black folks, it was not widely known that black folks in certain areas of the map needed more time under the sun to obtain the maximum amount of vitamin D needed to fight diseases like rickets in children and osteomalacia in adults. Other diseases associated with vitamin D deficiency include skeletal diseases, metabolic disorders, cancer, cardiovascular disease, autoimmune diseases, infections, cognitive disorders, and/or mortality. Many black folks simply adopted studies done for white folks.

There is a disproportionate number of racial minorities who have no insurance, are unemployed or underemployed, and are employed in jobs that do not provide healthcare insurance. Some are disqualified for government assistance programs and/or fail to participate because of administrative barriers.

Black folks are more likely to experience racial inequality in health care. This is so because discrimination will always persist in the United States since those systemic laws allowing institutionalized discrimination still have a stranglehold on the system. And the laws prohibiting racial discrimination are inadequate for addressing issues of institutional racial discrimination. So far, you can see for yourself that the U.S. legal system has been particularly reluctant to address issues of racial discrimination that result from policies and practices that have a disparate racial impact.

Do you ever wonder why a cross section of policy makers are dead set on repealing Obamacare? Though Obamacare, otherwise known as the Affordable Care Act, passed into law in 2010, conservatives continue to fight it at every opportunity, in the courts and in Congress. Do you know why?

Many conservatives (another euphemism for mostly Republicans) oppose it for the same reason that liberals (euphemism for mostly Democrats) favor it. The government, through the Medicaid expansion and the exchanges, subsidizes insurance coverage for the working poor by raising taxes on the rich.

Simply put, the conservatives want to paint a picture that they are rich and thus, are paying for subsidizing the health care for the people. That is a good argument if you buy into the swan song that the people of modest means are jobless-ne'er-do-wells who pay no taxes.

Conservatives tend to sell a false notion that they are not enthusiastic about redistribution. That is where the deceit lies. Conservatives hate redistribution when nonwhites and poor people are scheduled to participate in such a program. There are basically no loopholes to take advantage of to deny nonwhites participation, like in housing loans.

Remember mortgage loans and the subsequent inequalities in its implementation? Government creation of a body to give loans to buy a house is redistribution. It was a redistribution of wealth. Both whites and nonwhites contributed to that pot of wealth.

There is this widespread belief by conservatives that the main driver of the federal government's fiscal deficit is the soaring cost of health entitlements, like Medicare and Medicaid. One can argue that wars too do far more fiscal damage to the budget than social programs.

Some of the champions of Obamacare tend to claim that this law will improve the healthcare issues by encouraging innovative approaches to paying providers, which will bring about big efficiency gains. Conservatives are against such arguments. Some have said that Obamacare is a highway to killing grandmothers across America. That only served as propaganda on their part.

Conservatives have argued, and loudly too, against the law, that instead of driving efficiency gains, the guidelines and recommended approach to insurance will make nonsense of cost-savings. They say such innovative approaches will cost more as it expands. Conservatives have concluded that Obamacare will make matters worse. Instead of tackling the health entitlement problem, conservatives say, Obamacare will make matters worse.

As is expected, conservatives are saying that Obamacare is a move from less socialism to full-scale socialism. Is it not interesting that anytime poor people and every American get the opportunity to participate in a program, it is suddenly termed as "socialism" and/or "big government"?

When President Eisenhower said these words, "Every gun that is made, every warship launched, every rocket fired, signifies in the final sense a theft from those who hunger and are not fed, those who are cold and are not clothed," what do you think he was talking about? President Eisenhower was a politician and a Republican. A very good and humane Republican. Can you find his type today? Of course!

CHAPTER 23

Ivy League Schools

———

IF YOU OBSERVED OR EXPERIENCED it . . .

From their beginnings, first-graders who are nonwhites are assigned to schools lacking in quality. What this means is the same pattern of keeping a people down. It means nonwhites are trained very early in skills that are inferior and therefore, not needed in the labor market. It is a preparatory setup for failure now and in the future.

Whether or not the attendees of such schools are able to graduate does not confer superior skills needed to survive on their own. This is why it was suggested in another chapter that when you decide to acquire skills, acquire the type which can put food on the table right away after graduation. It is not wise acquiring some skill that only encourages you to go resume, application in hand, begging to be hired.

Sometimes, it is as if some schools were set up as a vehicle in achieving the downfall of their students. The students are prepped for failure.

These schools of little relevance promote dropout rates among blacks. Schools with much relevance have their students graduating at rates higher than the irrelevant schools. Schools of relevance produce the implementers of the capitalism dripping with waters of racism.

You can see the end results of the assignment of first-graders to schools lacking in quality. Using the statistics from the U.S. Census Bureau in 1974, 8.1 percent of people of color between the ages of

25–34 were college graduates, while 21 percent of whites in the same age bracket graduated. Remember, blacks are 12–13 percent of the total population. Bearing that in mind, you can now imagine the disadvantage and the disparity. If you want to talk about prepping a group to fail, this is it.

There has always been racism in the educational system in the United States like it is in health care and wealth distribution. The coinage *separate but equal* came into being for a reason. The problem is that you would want to think that after all those years, racism in the educational system would have come to a standstill.

You want someone to tell you that it is not so.

OK. It is not so.

If it is not so to you, it may be one of three reasons. You do not suffer discrimination, and/or you do not have the available statistics, or you just don't care.

Below are quotes from two eminent Americans. The first is a quote by a Supreme Court judge—Justice Antonin Scalia. The second is a quote/paraphrase from Donald Trump. Read both and decide for yourself. Be mindful to remember the earlier discussions on affirmative action.

> *"There are—there are those who contend that it does not benefit African Americans to get them into the University of Texas where they do not do well, as opposed to having them go to a less-advanced school, a less—a slower-track school where they do well.*
>
> *"One of—one of the briefs pointed out that—that most of the—most of the black scientists in this country don't come from schools like the University of Texas. They come from lesser schools where they do not feel that they're—that they're being pushed ahead in—in classes that are too fast for them."*

Scalia was referring to an amicus brief filed in the *Fisher vs University of Texas at Austin* case, which involved a white woman who was denied admission to the university and claims that the college's affirmative action policy is responsible.

Can you put your head around that statement? If you cannot, wait until you read Trump's quote. The quote is very important because he was not just referring to any American but a president. He is basically saying exactly the same thing as Judge Scalia, albeit in different words and context.

Hear Trump. Trump arguably is Penn's Wharton School's most famous alumni and billionaire, who received an undergraduate degree in 1968.

> *"I heard he was a terrible student, terrible. How does a bad student go to Columbia and then to Harvard? I'm thinking about it; I'm certainly looking into it. Let him show his records. I have friends who have smart sons with great marks, great boards, great everything, and they can't get into Harvard."*

This is a claim he's made in the past, but one he doubled down on by suggesting he's probing that area of the president's life.

Let us be honest here: Supreme Court Judge Scalia and Donald Trump were saying exactly the same thing, which is: How the hell did this black man end up on an Ivy League campus? Schools that are the reserve of white America.

The unfortunate truth is this: This is what obtains all over the place and those in charge of implementing policies know it too well. It just happened that two prominent Americans chose to wear their feelings on their sleeve.

So, what is the argument now? The argument is *affirmative action is bad*. The argument is that black folks cannot work themselves into Ivy League schools; therefore, they should be left in slow-track schools.

This is our postracial America.

I marvel at times at the writers of our policies at every level of government. I marvel at how they have everything systemically covered. First, from primary schools to high schools, schools in nonwhite communities are badly provided for in all aspects. You name it—be it experienced teachers or effective ones, minority-dominated schools have less. Be it in areas of decent infrastructures and a conducive atmosphere for studies. Not likely. Numerous studies point to insufficiencies.

It is no longer news that students in schools with a high concentration of minorities are more than twice as likely to have an ineffective teacher as students in schools with a low minority enrollment. They are being prepared for failure from the beginning.

And don't you love it when they complain about nonwhites who made it out of the hood to Ivy League schools? Don't you love it when, after all the odds, they make it to Ivy League schools? And we hear that pornography of a swan song again and again—only, this time, the song's title is "Affirmative Action."

Most Ivy League schools are still bedeviled by the same racist agenda of capitalism. You have to look sometimes to see and/or experience it. It is part of the setup inside the hidden barriers.

CHAPTER 24

The Representatives & NAACP

IF YOU UNDERSTOOD IT WELL . . .

Whether the leaders—our leaders—are Republicans or Democrats, racism and/or apartheid is still the norm. The leaders were/are confined to using laws legislated before they were born. Don't be deceived. Do not be swayed even by the sweet words of your local leaders. There cannot be an exercise of powers exceeding that which is in the Constitution. In the end, both parties are populated by those sponsored by the capitalists.

In the final analysis, both parties are comprised of representatives who continue to engage in systemic racism. That President B. Clinton now holds the record for incarcerating more blacks than the three presidents before him must mean something to you.

He is a president of the Democrat Party stock. He positioned himself very well with the minorities while doing the bidding of his Southern white folks. They cried "high crime rate," and he responded.

The recipients of his highhandedness are those who affectionately refer to him as the "black president." He rewarded them with the three-strikes law. President B. Clinton, single-handedly, destroyed many African American families. Fathers were torn from their families.

Grandfathers, sons, uncles, and friends were whisked off the streets to languish in the prisons for a mere $10 worth of crack or weed. He claims that he did not know that the three-strike law would affect nonwhites like it did.

Some would respond to that by the use of the parlance "talk to the hand."

If racism is a set of ideologies and practices that seek to justify, or cause, the unequal distribution of privileges or rights among different racial groups, then what is apartheid?

You choose one and that exactly is what President B. Clinton chose to do. He was listening to his white constituents while pandering to the black constituents. He even curried favor among the black representatives. The irony of it all is that some black leaders backed him.

Apartheid means a state of being apart. It means separate. Literally, it was a system of racial segregation enforced by legislation and force. Under apartheid, the rights, association, and movement of the people, usually blacks and other ethnic groups, are curtailed.

This is exactly what occurs in the United States. It has been colored. It has been cleverly colored into the laws. It is systemic. It is colored, whether as open as Jim Crow laws or as hidden as it is in the enacted voting laws in the South or as amended in the Constitution of the United States. They legitimized racism then, and racism is still legal today. Some would want to argue with that last sentence, but once you understand that capitalism is racism, your argument becomes dead on arrival.

Many people like to associate apartheid with South Africa. What about the USA, Botswana, Northern and Southern Rhodesia, etc.? Have you thought about those countries? Though some of the listed countries, including South Africa, have abandoned apartheid, the USA practiced separate but unequal. The USA and a few others still practice clever and systemic apartheid.

THE USE OF THE VOTING RIGHTS

Have nonwhites used this right effectively? For some nonwhites, the newest swan song is: Vote Democrat. It is always this song: Vote Democrat, as if Democrats were exonerated from their participation in the creation of the system.

If this crop of politicians wants to separate themselves from the Founding Fathers of slave owners and to plant new ideas for participation, the existing constitutional laws need a makeover or do over. That is the least they can do.

What effort are they making to rid the system of systemic laws that made the racism foundation stronger? Obviously, one cannot be asking such a question of both parties. One can try asking the party of the Clintons—the Democrats.

Democrats never made the lots of nonwhites any better, even as recently as the Bill Clinton administration. His administration was the creator of three-strikes—you are out! Obviously, he can claim now that he did not know then that black lives would be disproportionately affected by those laws.

Sometimes you wonder whether the black caucus of the Democratic Party was in a deep slumber while Bill Clinton was crafting the three-strikes, you are out law.

You can read all you need to know about the NAACP of old in the history books. They fought for freedoms—all freedoms for all. Once, I sat in a restaurant in New York. As I waited to be attended to, I noticed some pictures displayed on the walls. I particularly noticed the portrait with Dr. Kwame Nkrumah and Dr. Martin Luther King Jr. I don't know when that picture was taken, but I can guess it was late 1950s or early 1960s. Most of us were perhaps not on this earth then.

What struck me about those men was that both were leading the struggle to gain freedom. One was leading the struggle in America, and the other in Africa struggling against the same white men. Both men would be monitored and thwarted by the FBI and CIA, respectively.

I wondered if they both understood the struggle they were engaged in. I wondered if perhaps Dr. Nkrumah knew he would gain independence for his land—Ghana. It was clear-cut.

I am still wondering if Dr. Martin Luther King Jr. knew whether the struggle would still be ongoing decades later. Perhaps he knew it when he said, "I might not get there with you" for even if he were alive today, we would not still be there.

If Dr. King had plausible expectations, and how to get those expectations, the NAACP of today doesn't seem to understand how to pick its battles. Obviously, the plausible freedoms are dumbed down in well-planned and laid-out systemic laws. To this end, nonwhites and poor people in this society continue to be the piñatas of the rich.

That the NAACP was caught napping when President B. Clinton's three-strikes law was crafted and passed is unforgivable.

It does not seem to matter which political party is in power. Nonwhites are not only at the receiving end of discriminatory laws, they are now swimming in a river porn of racism, and, as usual, people pretend not to be watching. It is as if they are enjoying the orgies of discrimination.

For most of our lives' existence on earth, the voting patterns of mainly black voters can easily be anticipated. They have voted for the Democrats for as long as I have witnessed the voting cycles. I am wondering why. I enquired from many nonwhite peoples—some I knew, and others I did not know.

I can summarize all the answers I received by quoting an article by Madison Moore, titled "Why Do Black People Always Vote Democratic?"

"If there's one thing Grandma Moore always beat into my head, it's that I would be stupid if I voted for anyone outside of the Democratic

Party. Ever since I reached the legal voting age, my grandma has in-sisted that I choose the Democrat, whoever it was, no matter what. And this was way before there were viable black candidates. She re-spects my prerogative to think for myself, of course, but with a stern warning that I would be making a great big fool of myself if I voted for any other party. Like I would be committing cultural and ethnic treason by voting for people in the other party. Even if you don't know the issues, just vote for the Democrat," she told me

Grandma Moore could be any of your black friends or pastors. It is the same everywhere.

One other answer that's very interesting goes like this: It's purely economic.

Most black people have significantly lower incomes compared to many white people in the United States. That is a fact. The Democratic Party is one that undeniably promotes programs that tend to cater to the poor while the Republican Party tend to cater to corporations.

Though I will take this assumption as truth, with a pinch of salt, this has been the perception of some of the Democratic voters. Some of them erroneously believe or think that Democrats equal fighting for the poor, and Republicans equal standing with the rich and corporations.

The benefits that poor people receive has always been a legislated program that must be implemented, notwithstanding what party was in charge.

It has been this way for generations. Some think that the Democrats believe in bottom-up economic policies. And Republicans will quickly and derogatorily call that socialism. Categorizing anything as socialism is a political ploy the Republicans use when all of Americans, and not just whites, are to share in any government program.

Meanwhile, Republicans peddle the trickle-down economics pop-ularized by President Reagan. It simply means—deregulation, free

markets, tax breaks, open tax loopholes. Many economists will not hesi-
tate to point out the devastation such policies wrecked on our economy
during President Reagan's tenure. It was reckless then, as it would be
reckless today, if implemented.

Many poor people (black and white and in-betweens) vote Democrat
in greater numbers—at least in the recent past elections, because some
think it is in their economic interest to do so. At least, that was the
perception.

The truth of it is, notwithstanding what party is in charge—
Republican or Democrat, government programs will be maintained and
government benefits will be given no matter your political leaning as
long as you meet the criteria.

Does it really matter what party controlled the executive and legislative arms of government? That question was necessary because
the capitalists still have an iron grip on both parties. Capitalists set
up the system. They know how it works and how to manipulate it so
well.

Sometimes, it seems like the real power lies with capitalism. A political science lecturer is likely to tell you that in your vote lies the power.
We would like to believe that it is that simple.

It is, at times like these, that we wish that the voters own the media
and that the voters are also well informed. An uninformed voter can be
molded like the doughboy by the media. It depends on which media the
voter is listening to and who controls that medium.

The majority of poor people have been voting one way. Their votes
have not yielded rectification of the institutionalized discrimination.
Their votes have not made schools, medical care, or policing any better.
If anything, and if you are keeping note, their quality of life has gone
down steadily in all areas of measurement.

Indeed, incarceration of black people has climbed to its highest under a Democratic Party reign in the 1990s. And this, perhaps, is "better"

than the cocaine era epidemic of the 1980s and 1990s that practically destroyed black communities. Many black and poor lives were destroyed, and available statistical numbers were at best low estimates.

Many poor and African American families have struggled for generations with persistent poverty, especially in the inner cities. These conditions were further strained during the 1980s and 1990s by the widespread use of crack cocaine.

According to some estimates, between 1984 and 1989, the homicide rate for black males aged 14 to 17 more than doubled. The homicide rate for black males aged 18 to 24 increased nearly as much. Most people in policy-making positions looked away. It was a black people's problem. It was not America's problem.

At that period, the black community also experienced an 80 percent–100 percent increase in fetal death rates, low birth-weight babies, and weapons arrests. Most families were without both parents, and the number of children in foster care skyrocketed.

And then came the three-strikes, you are out law. Thus, in 1996, approximately 60 percent of inmates incarcerated in the U.S. were sentenced on drug charges, and you guessed who the culprits were—black men.

Thus, in the '80s, one party was preoccupied infesting black communities with crack cocaine and in the 1990s, the other party came in for the kill with the three-strikes, you are out law.

You see, what if you were told that the left wing and the right wing belonged to the same bird? Would it make sense then?

Either way, the poor are the losers. Are there really ideological opposites?

The three-strikes, you are out bill was a bill directed at "crime" all right. It was also the height of black lives shattered. It was an affirmation that black peoples' lives are not on par with other lives—including animals' lives.

It was the federal government's actions headed by Bill Clinton telling the states that they will receive more money if they punish people more severely.

More than half the states and the District of Columbia followed the money and enacted stricter sentencing laws for violent offenses.

It should be a good idea to protect law-abiding citizens. It is also a good idea to provide for those who, for years, have been prohibited from participation in our capitalism.

It is a good idea to present and communicate through the media that the government is protecting the citizenry. What is not a good idea is the implementation of an agenda that uses hidden barriers as a setup for systemic suffocation of a people under the guise of protecting its citizenry.

That was deceitful.

From available statistics, any reasonable and smart person will know immediately the communities the crime bill would impact most. One does not need any research to come to that conclusion. However, even if one wanted to be detailed with a backup of a study, there were available papers on incarceration in the United States.

To not have seen this clever attempt at strengthening the existing discriminatory laws can be equated to carelessness, sabotage of self, and outright negligence.

The attempt is simply to make fishers of black men of the bill. It is to gather people as raw materials for the privatized prisons. And you know who will constitute about 67 percent of the inmates . . .

If it was not planned, it turned out to be the perfect plan.

How can black leaders not see that this was a setup? Today, with every black baby born, there is a one in six chance (or worse) of getting arrested and ultimately spending some time in prison.

And if you happen to be born white through no fault of your own, your chance of going to prison is one in 17 and is getting better!

Just thinking about the motive for this bill and the outcome 20 years later makes you wonder what kind of leaders we sometimes elect. How any leader can come to terms with the unfairness of this law baffles a great many. It was as if the legislation was directed at black and nonwhites and generally poor persons of all colors.

Any reasonable person would argue that laws are not only a matter of fairness and justice, they should be a matter of national security too. The 1994 crime bill is misguided and simply callous.

Why would Bill Clinton not see that? Bill Clinton is not inherently wicked and out to minimize black peoples. Black peoples loved him. Was Bill Clinton that dumb and misguided? It is as if when black people think they have a choice, they find out later that they really don't have a choice under the setup.

The hidden barriers have a way of upstaging the choices. The choices are just between the two available evils. It's a bad cop/good cop situation.

Just like the good cop/bad cop playbook, the poor are just being played like a fiddle by the rich. The rich landowners . . . They call the shots. Their influence on policy makers, including presidents, is enslaving.

What was more misguided and unbelievably negligent was that the bill was initiated at the urging of the Republicans by a Democratic president. The so-called first black president who was overwhelmingly defended by black people, including Nelson Mandela during all his travails of impeachment.

Perhaps the Republicans can see a reason to play the good cop for a change. The 1994 crime bill did not sail through the Congress without the support of both parties. It was a windfall for the Republican Party, and they feel no remorse.

What will be a motivation for the Republican Party to work to minimize the Jim Crow-like laws? Perhaps winning some black votes will be more motivation than you might think.

Do not forget that it has been stated many times that it is cheaper to educate and train than to imprison. So, why do you think that policy makers chose to incarcerate more people in prisons over educating and training them?

Simply put, it is an all-time desire to keep a people down. No matter how good our country is, we still have the KKK and the KKK-minded persons in our midst. They are everywhere. Think of somewhere, and they are there. If you don't see them, it is because they are part of the hidden barriers.

They hide under the hoods because when they're done, they would want to return to being your police officers, your teachers, your doctors, your nurses, your senators, your mayors, judges, your counselors, your governors, your coworkers, and your whatever.

It appears the 1994 crime bill achieved more than the Ku Klux Klan (KKK) could ever have imagined to achieve.

By the end of Clinton's first term, the U.S. jails and prisons had added an additional 277,000 prisoners according to an *L.A. Time*'s article. If you did not know, that is more than twice as many prisoners added during Ronald Reagan's first term. Ronald Reagan did not give a rat's ass about the welfare of black people, yet he mustered the incarceration of only 129,000 prisoners—that means fewer blacks.

Our "first" black President Clinton, by January 2001, oversaw the addition of 673,000 new inmates to state and federal prisons. Ronald Reagan, in his bad '80s cocaine era, had only imprisoned 438,000.

The most troubling of the "first" black president's pretend performance is that nearly 60 percent of those imprisoned during his first 4 years were behind bars for nonviolent drug offenses. Yes, *nonviolent* crimes.

President Clinton's crime bill had a reverberating effect on black communities. As you can imagine, monies that should have been used to develop the poor was used to destroy them. As prison spending went up, the funding for programs that would help the disadvantaged declined.

President Clinton' s tough-on-crime posture to please the opposition led to the largest increase of the incarcerated in federal and state prison inmates in the history of any president of the United States. The sorry truth of it all is that black folks and nonwhites were at the receiving end.

Some argue that they were criminals, so they should the pay the price. If you argue along those lines, you absolutely do not understand systemic discrimination and racism.

Systemic racism is to quarantine a people from birth, and sometimes after death. Think about that for a minute.

There are those who cannot afford to put food on the table. For some, there is even no table to put the food on because for such a minor offense of a few ounces of weed (cannabis), the Clinton administration made it off-limits to benefit from any public benefits.

Black lawmakers cannot and should not be allowed to stay blameless in this devilish manipulation of bills to enhance already-existing systemic racist laws otherwise known as Jim Crow.

The NAACP must remember that he who calls for equity must come clean. The NAACP is neither blameless nor powerless. Was the NAACP forced to kowtow in the Democrat's agenda led by "black president" President Bill Clinton?

It sometimes feels like an invented reality, and most people accepted it as reality.

They were blindly behind President B. Clinton's invented reality. The so-called new Democrats joined hands with the president to promote bills banning drug felons from public housing and other public benefits, including those that help put food on the table.

If you really think about it, do real drug barons seek public housing or food stamps?

No matter how you answered that question, the question was an attempt to draw your attention to a real reality that this law was not really directed at real drug barons . . . but at minorities.

It was and still is a weapon to gather young black males into prisons and limit any ability for economic emancipation.

That bill which was ultimately signed into law by the "first black president" has automatically reversed all the freedoms of the incarcerated individuals. Their situation is worse than slaves of yesteryear.

They are the new face of America's new slavery.

If you looked up the definition of a felon, you may be surprised at what qualifies as a felony. The 1994 crime bill has made discrimination in all aspect of life—political, social, and economic very legal.

When you take a man's right to seek economic, political, and social power, when you take the same man's right to the benefits of food stamps, you have simply sissified that man.

The troubling advantage or disadvantage of wrapping oneself in a flag of the Donkey—the Democrat's mascot—is having a blind eye on the activities of all the parties. It is bad to slavishly support one party, just like it is to blindly believe for decades that the other party is out to get you. That is simply putting oneself in a position of perpetual disadvantage.

It is time to learn that in politics, and especially economics, there are no permanent foes or allies. This maxim applies to the black folks more now than ever before. A tilt in the voting pendulum of nonwhites to match those of independents might see yet a bigger carrot dangled by all parties seeking minority votes.

Some have argued that a divided house is easier to conquer. They have failed to embrace the maxim that people holed up in one house are easy pickings too.

It costs an average of $27,549 to hole up one prisoner a year. Currently, both state and federal prisons have approximately 2.2 million inmates.

It is a record-setting number following President Clinton's mandatory sentencing bill.

Now, that is a lot of resources that goes into wasting human resources. But because somebody, somewhere, determined that they want America to know that the government was tough on crime and criminals, they approved the unthinkable.

The hypocrisy of some politicians manifests their racism. Try as much as they would want to hide their racist agendas, they knew that the 1994 crime bill was targeting mostly blacks. If that was not racism, I wonder what is.

Almost always, when nonwhites are the targets of bad laws, policy makers turn blind eyes. As soon as the repercussions of keeping a blind eye starts to manifest in mostly white communities, the rhetoric and communication style changes dramatically.

The society shaped the judges, magistrates, police, teachers, etc., who are in our courts, our precincts, our colleges, and every other sphere of endeavor. Gangs are also the product of the society. Such gangs could be the KKK or any other, whether they are in college or on the streets; it does not make a difference. It is freedom of association. And they are proud to associate. Our police also enjoy the freedom of association like everybody else.

There is no denying or coloring the fact that some very few of them would be influenced by their prejudices while engaged in their official duties. Police in the South were originally established to catch and discipline fleeing slaves. That role has not changed, even though the job description uses other fancy words. The biases are the same. The same media influences the office holders like they influence the general populace. They may not directly accept the impact of such media influence.

You can, however, see that influence when the police make a description of an event—perhaps a criminal event. Their choice and use of words jive with the media's. They have learned well from the media. Like the media, they have mastered the art of making monsters out of black men. When the police see a monster, they are justified to put it down. They have prepared your mind through the media to accept it.

There is a reason why the prison population in America is higher than anywhere else in the world, including China. The prison population in the United States is greater than the populations of the 17 smallest nations on earth. It is as if the intent for the prisons' large population is premeditated. And, of course, it *was* premeditated. Remember only one premeditation: the 1994 crime bill.

Does it even bother anyone in the states where marijuana is now legal, that some significantly rich white men are now poised, standing in line to run big marijuana businesses after many years of locking up black men and women for doing less than the same?

Even now that it is legal, black folks are almost excluded from participation, like they were excluded from participating in capitalism. And you ask why black men are frustrated?

Only a foolish black man would be sane under these circumstances.

Many would want to blame President Bill Clinton. Some even want to blame Clinton's wife—Hillary. I hope this does not only expose the NAACP and the black leadership but also President B. Clinton. Whom exactly does the Democratic Party account to?

Would you seriously believe that Bill Clinton did not consult fully with the black leaders? Now they want to blame every gaffe on the "first" black president. Shame.

The NAACP must account for the role it played in the enacting of a bill that decimated and still decimates the black community. The NAACP, perhaps by an act of dereliction of responsibilities, sold her people into the hands of those whose intention it has always been to continue to decimate the black folks in America.

CHAPTER 25

Criminalization of African Americans

TRANSLATING AMERICA . . .

You create a monster, and then shoot it. It has always been a good tactic. If you want to kill a people, you first kill their reputation.

Have you been walking on the streets, any street in the USA, and suddenly there is a group of young black men walking toward you? No matter how badly you react, it is going to be directly proportional to how much you have listened to and believed the picture that has been painted of black people.

You have lived through daily repetitions of negative sounds and images of black men.

It is the conditioning of all liberal minds that would ordinarily oppose any and all impending carnage on anyone or on any group of people. What this means is: Give a dog a bad name. When you kill it, people will feel good that a mad dog is no longer on the streets.

What, then, is better than making a monster out of them? If you succeed in making the majority of people to believe that a group of people are monsters, the people will happily embrace, or at least not frown at, the systemic elimination of such monsters. It is not new. History has documentaries of such behaviors all over the continents.

Even the Bible had a good example. Egypt made monsters of the Jews. What the Bible failed to say was that the Jews were Egyptians until God, alias Yahweh, decided to show His face.

Like any good branding when you brand, it sticks, especially when you brand day in, day out. The media was at it as if their existence depended on branding black people. They made monsters of black people. White skin was branded as superior in the Americas and the world.

If you are one that believes that white skin is better, you have some serious psychological issues. If you also think that black is better, you are in the same boat of insanity. You may have a B.Sc. in engineering, but your ignorance stinks. Perhaps you have bought into the media's insanity or some form of indoctrination.

It may not be your fault. The branding was working.

The American media is very good at branding. From radio to TV to Disneyland and Hollywood, they are masters at branding, especially the branding of black folks. Branding has been taken to a level of: If you are a privileged kid, you are better off seeing a counselor to mitigate your devils, whereas, if you are poor or of a minority race, you are better off being counseled . . . in the four walls of a prison.

In America everything is categorized. For census purposes, people are categorized. If you want to fill out an application for a job, you are asked whether you are white or black or other. It is all about categorization. It is about racism. You are classified as minority or majority, male or female, married, single, or have a significant other. Your classification and zip code determine how much you pay for insurance, your mortgage, etc., and how, almost always, you turn out in life.

Why is there such a thing as a "racist" classification in a "civilized" country? There should be just a country, not a country of classified citizens.

Up until recently, the roles reserved for black folks in Hollywood was that of serving the white man. In fact, the black man had been so well branded, even housewives who commit murders have learned to blame it on the black man.

Even amateurs got into it. Some white suspects deflect suspicion and point police in the direction of black monsters. In 1994, a white murderer, Susan Smith, a mother in Union, South Carolina, claimed that a man had commandeered her car with her two kids—Alex, a 14-month-old, and Michael, a 3-year-old.

In her mind, she created a suspect—a carjacker—a black male in his late 20s to early 30s, wearing a plaid shirt, jeans, and a toboggan-type hat. The media ran with the story.

"It's a black monster."

The composite of her description was published in major newspapers nationwide. Later, Susan Smith appeared on national television, tearfully pleading with the supposed black man to return her kidnapped sons, unharmed. I can still see the rerun of that video in my mind's eye. The entire nation empathized with her.

The major words that remained so true to type was that of a reverend. The Reverend Mark Long—the pastor of the church where the Smiths attended services. He said in reference to the black suspect as he painted an image of the black monsters, "There are some people that would like to see this man's brains bashed in."

There you have it.

The truth of the matter was that Susan Smith would later confess to the murder of her two children all by herself. There was no black man/monster involved.

You would want to believe that the saddest part of that saga was Susan Smith's nonapology to black folks after apologizing to her dead sons in her letter of confession. Oh no!

That the media played along and believed Susan Smith—the usually clean, white woman, was the saddest part of the saga. How can any smart person believe that a black man would kidnap kids that are not his? How was he going to feed those kids with a nonexisting job and a jail he was soon to be behind? In the rush to announce to the world how good they were at branding black folks, the media jumped into the mud with Susan Smith.

It was the black folks who separately started to hint to the police to ask the woman more questions. This was because it was absolutely out of character for a black man to go kidnapping white kids. If it was a carjacking, that may have been partially logical, but then the kids would be left where they could be found.

That is a sublimely self-attestation to presenting black folks' behaviors. Nonwhites have been painted worse than this, and they seem to have accepted the taint.

And they are not zooming out of those caricatures they make of other races fast enough as some experiments have shown using little kids. These are the experiments where kids of different races are exposed to illustrations of children of different races or dolls made to look like babies from various races.

Irrespective of the race of the children, they seem to cling to the brandings of the media, which suggests negativity for certain racial groups like the society they live in. For the record, some of the kids, including African Americans and Hispanics, chose the white kids as the "good kid."

One poignant highlight in one of the experiments that is sure to bring a few tears to a parent's eyes was when the black girl had to identify the doll she closely resembles. She correctly identified the black doll. This was the same doll she had assessed earlier, as "bad," "ugly," and "unruly."

The subliminal message in whatever form starts early. The torment lasts a long time. The self-despise once inflicted is a job well done, and it is priceless for those doing the damage.

Do you now see why some news channels start their breaking news with headlines such as:

a. Some "thugs" instead of some "people" . . .
b. A "black" man murdered . . . instead of a "man" murdered . . .
c. The criminal was described as a "black" man, 6 feet tall, and wearing a hoodie, and the police were reportedly scared for their lives . . .

Have you witnessed a protest recently?

If you understand the mind-set of those that control the media, you can tell from the reporting without watching the videos on TV who are in the civil unrest. You can tell if they are white or nonwhites.

If they are nonwhites, you start to hear the words—"lawlessness, thugs, criminals, wild animals, looting, bad guys, destructive, looters."

You start to hear the media ask questions. The audacity to ask racist questions knows no boundaries. Perhaps they too are suffering from mental slavery. They do not know that the questions give them away as racists.

Like mental slavery, they are unaware of their racism. The irony of it all is that they do not even know or believe that they are asking discriminatory questions. Questions like—

a. Where are the black leaders?
b. Where are the community leaders?
c. Where are the pastors?
d. Where are the police?
e. Why are the police not in battle-ready fatigue with machine guns?
f. The police are standing by and are not doing anything.

If the rioters were whites who just decided to go on rampage because their team lost a game—you hear soft, kind words from the same media houses. Words like "young, fans, venting their frustrations, passionate, unfortunately, maybe, they're a little bit, just a bit out of control, it is tough to lose, they are just dancing on top of a car, it's civil unrest," etc.

Sometimes, the media seems to be reading a script when the rioters are mostly white folks. They do not even call it a riot. They say, "It's a party." The media uses phrases like "party gone awry" when the neighborhoods are under siege. Did I just use "siege"? OK, that was my word.

The media would never say that the city is under siege when white rioters are involved. Such words are used for black protesters. Other popular descriptive words for white riots and rioters are "party became a bit too rowdy." Sometimes they describe a riot as a "dispute, altercation," or "a brawl."

In all of these, cars and other properties were set on fire. In some instances, lives were lost. In those instances, they described it as some kind of "dispute that ended in some type of altercation."

While the "white rioters" are executing the riot, most often, a few police officers would be standing far off observing as if they were the spectators. No shooting, no military-type gear to show force—as is usually done for black protesters protesting racism.

The surprising thing about this double standard is that the police and the media tend to speak the same language when describing and/or covering rioters and crimes. In Waco, over 170 people were arrested while nine died. It was described as "some kind of altercation" (Waco Shootout: Biker Brawl at Twin Peaks Leaves Nine Dead).

In the Baltimore riots of 2015, there were zero deaths during the protest. But the protesters were described as "thugs, looters, arsonists," and "criminals."

If you go back in history, in the not-so-distant past, specifically during Hurricane Katrina, the word "looting" became the media's and the police's favorite word. It became the word to make monsters out of a people—a group of people.

The word was strategically used to demonize looters—all looters—so you might think. But it soon became an inflammatory word that was equated with rampaging, marauding hordes, lawlessness, vandalism, animals, thugs, and all the other clichés we have learned from many disaster movies and the overwrought media coverage of disasters and unrests nationwide.

In the chaotic and deadly days after Hurricane Katrina hit, orders circulated through the New Orleans Police Department. It was and still is a chilling message. The message simply meant that *private property would be prioritized over human life.* "Shoot them. Shoot the lousy looters." "Take our city back!"

It was the same rhetoric during the Ferguson and Baltimore protests. The message was, "Do what you have to do"—to contain the animals. It was the same scripted mandates that led to the deaths of people. It was simply a message that said—private properties are more valuable than some lives.

Some years later, another devastating hurricane tore through the U.S., leaving unimaginable destruction along its path. It left tens of thousands homeless and many more in desperate need of food and basic supplies.

But soon, the media's focus was removed from the devastation after a few scattered reports. The specter of the demon looter reemerged as the fodder for the firebrand pundits, especially on a particular news outlet.

The media, as always, is the voice of its masters. Such disasters are the opportunities for branding, and the media never fails to seize them.

It is an opportunity to choose one or more videos for repeat broadcasting. Most often, it is the video of a black person "looting." It usually is one scene repeated over and over again.

Where some black folks were found taking a few cans of soda and an accompanying cellophane bag, they were dubbed "looters."

The white folks were described as "finders" and the item dubbed the "find." The troubling question was—how did the media persons know who were looters and who were the finders of the items?

You see, once the DNA of racism was planted, it naturally germinated and grew enormously. The capitalists were watering and fertilizing it through the media. Everyone claims that they are not racist. That makes one wonder where the racism is coming from.

Racism has its ways of manifesting itself. A little watering and it blossoms. A few politicians understand the art of watering racist seeds.

The racial biases of the reporters in New Orleans have been alarming as well as it was shocking, yet they were on full display since Hurricane Katrina hit. They were not letting up. There was, however, one reporter whose reports flowed with the milk of human kindness, truth, and reason—Anderson Cooper. Anderson worked for the news outlet CNN. At one point, Anderson Cooper had seen enough of the deception and the accompanying lies. He differed with a politician—an act journalists are restrained from.

As if the media were in a competition, the reporters repeatedly referred to white folks as victims clinging to life. They were described as "survivors" whose residences had been devastated.

The African Americans going through the same devastations were portrayed in the opposite light. They were "looters" and "criminals." Most often, a scene of rowdiness in the stadium where the majority of black folks had converged was repeatedly shown on the news.

They portrayed the whole community of people in that stadium as lawless. Who in their right mind does not know that where there is multitude of people, there is bound to be disagreements and brawls?

It was a fight for survival.

It was human instinct.

The reporters disseminated these stories as if they had a clearinghouse—a sort of "Vatican"—where the news is scripted for onward transmission to news outlets.

They sound and read the same. While the humanizing and heartbreaking stories feature white victims and their families, videos of African American unruly crowds were incessantly and repeatedly played so as to brand.

Once you fall for those stories, you are sold. Do not be deceived. Some of the reporters are minorities too, who have a family to feed. So what if they had to be the master's voice? It was hard enough getting the job anyway in the first place.

It, therefore, wasn't any surprise that while victims of the flood were struggling to survive by any means necessary, some police officers were busy shooting to protect property. There were 11 fatalities.

Black folks have come to the understanding that for the branding of regular struggling white folks to make sense even to white folks, there must be in the background of a video of a rowdy crowd—black folks, of course—during discussions of some criminal or other activities that make the white folks feel good about themselves. It has always been like that, especially since poor white slaves had been removed and set on a new pedestal from their black counterparts.

The people (rich landowners—now the corporations) doing the manipulation of the branding know that to keep the regular "hardworking" whites folks happy, they have to remind them that they are better positioned on that ladder created since the Irish and other poor white descendants had been removed from the same chains of slavery that the black man still struggles with today.

We are still talking about the United States. Categorization is a subtle form of branding to engender divide and conquer on every facet of human activities. It is the same tactics employed by the landowners.

One of the things we learned from Hurricane Katrina was that the people in charge of affairs need to prioritize human lives over private property. They need to understand that most people behave with generosity, altruism, and solidarity in a disaster.

In disastrous situations, even those taking things from the wreckages of a warehouse or grocery store may be engaging in what is necessary for animal and human survival.

CHAPTER 26

Enter Barack Obama

———

BARACK OBAMA WAS THE 44TH president of the United States. In a speech on the Senate floor, the senator—Mitch McConnell—proclaimed that the first agenda of his party was to make the new president a one-term president.

Ordinarily, such rhetoric would be looked upon as the usual Washington politicking, but it was not just politics. It was a real threat. The fear of a black president was real just like the fear of the black man.

Reports have it that as Obama was being inaugurated in Washington, DC, a group of white Republicans—men at the other end of aisle, were gathered somewhere in the Capital plotting on strategies to make governing impossible for the new president.

It was a plot on how best to obstruct a yet-to-be-sworn-in president-elect. Of course, they thought it was in their best interest.

If you were in their shoes, perhaps you would be fearful too.

Perhaps if black folks had been running the show all those years, perhaps if it were black legislators, representatives, presidents, and judges that had passed all those discriminatory laws to make their grip on capitalism unshakeable, they would be planning to obstruct the first white president too.

The election of Barack Obama was an event not thought possible, at least not at the time it did. Some of the custodians of the racist culture did not envisage this happening. Truth be told, very few Americans envisaged the election of a President Obama.

It was like a wrest of power. So you can see the dilemma of those that participated in that meeting to plan strategies of obstruction.

In that meeting, it was agreed that if Obama wanted it, they were to say no even if it was what the Republicans had wanted over the years. Some call it politics, but it was not. It was the same fear that made a few men form a capitalist system of an economy using black people as its base and labor.

Mitch McConnell—a Republican, was the face of the opposition to President Obama. He was positioned to be the voice of the Republican positions. There were a few other faces like Rep. Eric Cantor. Eric Cantor's stubborn unwillingness to negotiate issues made him perhaps a Tea Party hero. Eventually, he became a Republican Party pariah and lost his nomination.

Those who really know, knew that the Republican position of saying no to the new black president was borne out of the same racist fear that the "Founding Fathers" had. They had a fear that a President Obama would embark on the task of removing systemic racism. This fear will drive the Republicans to become extremists.

They would not see themselves as such, but their subsequent actions brought the Congress to a standstill. They, thus, propagated the false maxim that "nothing good comes out of President Obama." They used their communication arm of the media to foist fear and hate across the nation.

Have you heard the slogan, "Let's take our country back"? When you hear it, how does it make you feel? Take your country back? From whom? Do you see the blatant racism that goes for political campaigns?

Everyone but the racist knew why the Republicans were up in arms. Even a president—Jimmy Carter—knew it was all about racism. Jimmy

Carter claimed that much of the opposition to Obama had arisen because the president is black. It was not that black folks and President Obama were waiting for a rubber stamp from Congress. They already know that racism pervades everything American—even the presidency. Anyone who follows political events at Capitol Hill anticipates push back from the opposition, not the outright block to debates that were rampant during the Obama presidency.

President Carter just nailed it—this time.

In one of their articles on September 16, 2009, theguardian.com had this on former President Jimmy Carter: *"The former president said racism had come to the surface across the country because of a belief held by many whites that an African American is not qualified to be in the White House. I think an overwhelming portion of the intensely demonstrated animosity toward President Barack Obama is based on the fact that he is a black man, that he's African American."*

According to the paper, "The Republican Party today issued a denial, saying Carter was 'flat-out wrong,' and that opposition was not because of Obama's skin color but his policies."

The article went on to quote President Carter again: *"And that racism inclination still exists. And I think it's bubbled up to the surface because of the belief among many white people, not just in the South but around the country, that African Americans are not qualified to lead this great country. It's an abominable circumstance, and it grieves me and concerns me very deeply."*

And by the way, this was about the same period white Republican Congressman Joe Wilson shouted, "You lie!" during Obama's key speech to the Congress.

Most Americans saw that event take place on live TV—a white man yelling to the first black president of the United States, "You lie!" In-your-face kind of racism cannot get any worse than that.

It was a stride President Obama rode throughout his presidency.

If you can ask yourself, notwithstanding your color, black or white—would you like to be treated the same way black folks had been treated for hundreds of years? That was a wonderful line I heard somewhere on social media. Perhaps you too, like others, have come to the understanding of how powerful and strong the social media is.

A Republican, Mr. Lawrence Wilkerson, former chief of staff to Colin Powell, put it like this: "Let me be candid: My party is full of racists. And the real reason a considerable portion of my party wants President Obama out of the White House has nothing to do with the content of his character, nothing to do with his competence as commander in chief and president, and everything to do with the color of his skin. And that is despicable."

Would you have time to compare those words to President Carter's comments?

Even Bill Clinton described Obama's bid for the Democratic Party nomination for the president as "The biggest fairy tale I have ever seen." That, for many black people, was the turning point, if they ever had doubts as to who to vote for between Hillary and Barack.

Bill Clinton knew what he was talking about. He is a Southerner. He understood how the game was played. If you don't know the real America, you are bound to be shocked. If you don't understand the real America, you will be angry. And many Americans were angry, and that statement, among other things, cost the Clintons the Democratic primary of 2008.

Today, America has not changed much from the days of Jim Crow laws. They just got rid of the superfluous cosmetics of Jim Crow while applying other types of cosmetics that are barely noticeable. The new cosmetics are as devastating, or worse, than the old Jim Crow.

When President B. Clinton thus said ". . . a fairy tale . . ." it aroused a deeper feeling of exasperation that nonwhites have been made to feel over the years. They have heard the "black president" loud and clear.

President B. Clinton understood the South's history then and now. He understood that in the South and in some towns like Greenwood, Mississippi, even to this day, they can have a separate portion of a restaurant made ready for where black folks can eat in.

It does not matter that the time clock read the year AD 2016. It is just how it is, even when there is no law mandating such segregation. It is a learned culture from Jim Crow.

So, those who use the word "fairy tale" when a black man is running for president of the United States of America use it as a code.

Those who the message was intended for hear and understand the codes in the messages.

Have you ever heard your white Republican colleagues and, of course, Democrats, for that matter, speak in codes? Have you ever heard anyone speak in codes? There are code words used everywhere, especially when the intended target is black or nonwhite.

Here are a few:

"He is a breath of fresh air . . ." because he's saying everything white folks think at night.

"Let us take our country back . . ." Even though this code had been used before, it sounds awkward, especially after almost 8 years of President Barack Obama.

"Let us make our country great again . . ." Was our country not great before and during Obama? It will still be great after Obama. It will be even greater if we dismantle racism.

"He is well-spoken . . ." A phrase reserved for the praise of supposedly black candidates. Blacks are supposed to be thugs and monsters who weren't expected to speak well.

There are so many "aha!" moments to nail coded words in our language. However, many of us seem to play dumb & dumber to the codes. This nation has had an ugly past and some truths, that in 2016 we are no further ahead on race relations than we were 100 years ago, are a manifestation of the deep-rooted systemic discrimination.

That Barack Obama was elected president does not change the script, just like the election of Benazir Bhutto as Pakistan's prime minister did not change the attitude toward women, nor does Oprah Winfrey's billionaire status negate blacks' poverty.

When Barack Obama became President Barack Obama, expectations were high. It was normal. It was especially highest among people of color, some of whom, like some white folks, hardly understood the workings of government.

Some believed the new president had enormous powers. The Congress (at least part of it) saw to it that the first black president did little to cause any imbalance in the setup.

The obstructionist policy of most elected Republican representatives has continued to the last months of President Obama's second term.

In the last year of President Obama's presidency, the Republicans vowed that any nomination to replace Judge Scalia would not be looked into, much less talk of confirmation, no matter how qualified. Recall that Judge Scalia had died suddenly. The move by the Republicans was nothing but the same old racist plan agreed upon to obstruct this president.

Some will put a spin on it. They spin the move in very many directions, one being that a confirmation of Obama's nominee will give the left a majority in the highest court.

The truth for the Supreme Court is that at any given time, one side is always going to have the majority.

So that argument does not hold water. If anything, it shows the desperation on the part of those swimming in the pool of racist politics— politics of "if Obama wants it, just say no."

Have you heard of such moves in recent politics? Of course, racism is communicated in various ways, and those doing the communication would be quick to tell you that they (Republicans) impeached President Bill Clinton—a Southern white man.

What they are trying very hard to communicate is that since they did it to Bill Clinton, that covers their racist gestures to Barack Obama. They will quickly follow up on that argument and tell you that they did worse to President Clinton because he was impeached.

They will not tell you that they convened a meeting whose main purpose was to frustrate a black president, thus, frustrating America, *even before he was sworn in.* We all know politics when we see it, and we understand racist politics even when it is dressed in flavorings of hidden barriers in the setup.

Racism is indeed evil.

That brings us to this question. If capitalism was built on the back of racism and allowed to thrive in the United States, must subsequent generations live by the mistakes of our forefathers? The mistakes are too costly to ignore.

But do you really blame the Republicans for the refusal to schedule a hearing for the Supreme Court nominee? It could be suicidal and a political malpractice to schedule a hearing. It seems like with all the shenanigans, they have succeeded in maneuvering their party into a difficult and complicated position. The way out is maintaining a numerical lead in both houses and/or win the presidency. Both are very difficult to accomplish.

Republicans are fighting for survival.

Their racist plans of obstruction are more self-obstructing to the party than it is to Obama. Their plans to not do something has backfired on the Republican establishment. The extent of self-inflicted injuries was evident in the 2016 Republican presidential primaries. Whether they can recover is a matter of tactics and time.

Obama has almost single-handedly and not by doing anything particularly, eviscerated the Republicans, the same particular thing they feared most. They played their hand of fearmongering so much so that their fears became self-fulfilled.

This is a testament to the "no-drama Obama" concept. He watched them shout themselves hoarse and ultimately self-destruct.

Perhaps President Obama was more than prepared for the presidential tasks and battles. They did not call him "no-drama Obama" for nothing. Barack Obama, the person, is known for being eloquent and articulate. He is an excellent public speaker. All you need to do to find out how gifted a speaker he is, is to watch a video of any of his campaigns.

During the 2008 campaigns, the media was used to describing him as calm and calculated. He rarely gets upset, even while confronting a crisis—a trait he put to use when the political enemies went to town to dig about his religion, church, and birth certificate, or when the Republicans continued their obstructionist tactics and name-calling.

He is determined and self-confident, as can be noticed throughout his life. That he decided to run for president against all odds is a testament to his self-assuredness and confidence.

When he decides on a goal, and even where all the circumstances were not very favorable, his confidence shone through and carries him to success. Perhaps some of us were witnesses and/or beneficiaries of his legacy.

CHAPTER 27

The Conclusion

———

AT THIS POINT, WE SHOULD all be familiar with the landowners—those you might refer to as the elite. Some people call them bourgeois, while politicians love to berate them as the 1-percenters. Sometimes they are the corporations. You know the landowners, no matter the name they are called.

Though the politicians would want you to believe that they berate the top 1 percent, it is these elites—the 1 percent—that controls everything, your politicians included. They hold the majority of America's wealth and prosperity.

When money speaks, stupid walks. It has always been like that, and there is no change in sight. The landowners will keep it that way because they invented the line of argument that says, "When money speaks, truth is silent." To them, truth is a prisoner in their world—this earth.

In fact, they own the earth's wealth. The wealth includes every resource—natural or human. Remember that they owned humans as slaves in the not-so-distant past.

Today, they make you go to wars just to protect their wealth. They sell to you all those jingles about patriotism and your way of life and how you must protect it. They do all these through their communication department—the media—and you fall for it hook, line, and sinker, like most average-thinking people would.

You have just been played for a sucker, like others before you had been played. It's a cycle.

That there is a global elite in the first place is a suggestion of an imbalance in the economic well-being levels of peoples around the globe. If we are all human—as we all are—is it too much to ask for the economic well-being for all?

Are we so trapped and caged within a system where a select few lord it over the masses, and the masses sit there lamenting their low-level economic standing while happily taking commands from their lords? You bet. You are part of the masses that take orders.

You wake up at 5 a.m. and get ready for a job. It is a weekly routine. You happily do this job until you are unable to wake up and go to that job again. By the time you realized it, you are too old to do anything about it. You have been had. Perhaps you have some savings, and you think that will give you some respite.

Just wait and see.

Some will end up smoking away their savings. The smokes are provided by the 1-percenters.

Some will end up drinking away their savings. The booze is manufactured by the 1-percenters.

Some will get addicted to drugs and all that other stuff. Never mind, the drugs are controlled by the 1-percenters.

They just sucked all your savings if you had any, and now, they are done with you. It does not matter what country you live in. The 1-percenters control the world.

Perhaps, a thought for a utopian community is just that—utopian. The creation of imbalance and inequality is a well thought out plan by the elite. There is this "hidden" weapon that has sustained the system— the thought that we have reached the best of a utopian society since many think that the "utopian society" is unattainable. Therein lies the weapon. What this means, therefore, is that different people, societies, have their own definition and levels of what constitute "utopia."

There is an imbalance because most of us don't care about having a choice in whether to participate in the system. To some, the system is rigged, so to attempt to participate in the system, some will argue, is already defeatist because the system was/is based on rules, structure, conditions, and limitations that encourage and empower the elite to structure the societies to create an illusion of perfection.

Such perception of perfection is so strong that many societies accept it as the level of a utopia. Of course, it is rigged but more so in some societies than others. If you understand how the elite has manipulated the system, you will see that its foundation is anchored on inequality.

Thus, inequality is created where none existed. It has nothing to do with races or tribes. It has nothing to do with the color of your skin. This is why this writer has issues with the way racism as a word is employed and used. I'd better use the word "hate."

It only looks like racism in the United States because racism was cheaper to implement via segregation. It was more or less a divide-and-conquer strategy. It was a . . . *we against them* tactic. The end desire is the same. The 1-percenters are still at the top controlling how you eat, dress, socialize, etc. The elites are elite for a reason—they are very cunning and smart. Some of them had an early start in the accumulation of wealth through lineage, etc.

The worst form of being is not knowing you are a mental slave to the controllers of the societies we live in. There are many who think they have freedom, but what you have is nothing near that. The other worst part of being is not being able to see that you are still under bondage.

Those (landowners or corporations) that set the agenda—rulers of your societies—will do and tell us things we would readily accept as all right because we, the majority of the peoples, do not know any better.

It does not matter whether you are black, white, Asian, Arab, etc. Your thinking is controlled. They do it through the news, movies, commercials, music videos, TV and reality shows . . . you name it—there are various creative ways to reach you unless you are in a cave. You are likely to believe that this media bombardment is created for informative and entertainment purposes only—and that is the "truth" they want you to believe anyway. But that is wholly not true. The real truth is that they are subliminally telling you what to think or learn.

What they don't want you to know is that the media is the most effective way to program the human mind. Those who do the programming are highly paid specialists in their fields. The landowners have the means to possess the best minds to do their bidding.

In their minds, they have figured long ago the power of subliminal messages through suggestion. They understand how powerful thoughts are.

They have also figured out long ago that perception is everything.

Even in the face of being the country with the highest incarceration rate in the world, you can now begin to see the illusion created of the United States as the "land of the free." And the world, including most African Americans, have that perception too. The quote below is appropriate here:

"Mental slavery is the worst form of slavery. It gives you the illusion of freedom, makes you trust, love, and defend your oppressor, while making an enemy of those who are trying to free you or open your eyes."

In a 1937 speech in Menelik Hall, Nova Scotia, Canada, Marcus Garvey said:

"We are going to emancipate ourselves from mental slavery because whilst others might free the body, none but ourselves can free the mind."

The trouble is that most people do not see themselves as mental slaves in need of emancipation. They simply resist it and entrench themselves deeper in bondage.

Mental slavery is more damaging with lasting impacts than physical slavery because whereas the latter is imposed by force and by man from outside the person, the former comes from within. When a man suffers from mental slavery, all the subliminal messages would work on your soul.

At this juncture, let me ask this. Do you remember the song— "Redemption Song"—by Bob Marley?

Can you remember the part that goes like this—

". . . Emancipate yourselves from mental slavery; none but ourselves can free our minds . . ."

As you can see, the secret to freedom is in the education of the citizens— *all* the citizens, whereas the weapon for a maintained tyranny lies in keeping the people as ignorant as possible. That is a big problem.

There is, however, a bigger problem. The question arises of how we would know that we don't know, that we are afflicted with mental slavery in the first place. The logic is—if we are born into an invisible slavery system located in an arena of hopelessness, poverty, fear, and negativity, how would we be able to recognize mental slavery if this is all we have come to live by, from lineage to lineage, down the chain? And herein lies the biggest problem of all.

Your first attempt at emancipation is to experience a culture outside that which had you caged. The moment you experience freedom; you will know it.

Your attempt to understanding is, first, to understand how free you are in a society. Are you being treated like everybody else regardless of income, race, and zip code?

While recognizing how your society was set up to operate, do you take out your frustrations on those representing the authorities? Have you understood that the behaviors of law enforcers are shaped by society?

Does this affect your attitudes toward law enforcement? Should your perception, if negative, be channeled at the politicians or some other authority?

The idea here is not for you to hate the police. It is for you to be smart, or smarter, in dealing with those whose priority it is to reduce your numbers by any means necessary.

Until you get that simple logic, no one can help you, as you might end up as part of the statistics. You have to learn how to stay alive first. You may be killed while arguing or not arguing with those charged with policing us. Stay alive first!

One in three African Americans will be arrested for doing exactly the same thing as a white American. That was a paraphrase of Hillary Clinton on a campaign trail in a debate in an Ohio town meeting.

This is not a call for change in behavior because there is nothing wrong with your behavior. At some point in American history, there was a class of people who have said "yes sir" and "yes ma'am" to every beck and call by the master, yet such good behavior did not save them from lynching, hanging, and castration.

The idea is to stay alive today to fight another day.

The one thing that must be done always is to vote. Yes. Voting is part of the answer to most of the systemic laws. You vote and hold the politicians accountable. When you vote for a candidate and do not hold that candidate to account because s/he belongs to a particular party, you are not doing yourself or anyone any favors.

The Civil Rights Movement for African Americans and other people of color (NAACP) met seemingly unbeatable and sometimes vicious opposition. Some made the ultimate sacrifice. Some civil-rights activists and leaders, who included black, white, and Jews, were murdered.

They sacrificed so that we can enjoy the voting rights without dying on the streets like they did.

And justice to their cause prevailed.

They fought to extend constitutional rights and protection to the excluded. They won the battles for all Americans to get involved and to speak up. We can only honor their memories by going to the polls to choose our leaders.

To stand by and be a passive participant in elections is an injustice to the memories of those who suffered and died for these rights. Perhaps your lot is not any better today because they are passive or a one-time voter who hardly holds the elected to account.

If you don't vote for your district attorney or state attorney, you may not know it, but you are part of the reason we have 2.2 million people in jails in 2016.

You are part of the reason the black man is six times more likely than whites to wind up in jail. You may want to object to that, but if you knew your vote determined who appointed the judges, a judge who might stand in *your* trial someday, would you go and vote?

If you knew your vote determined who will appoint the police commissioner who assigns how officers and men would police or overpolice your streets, would you go out and vote? If you knew your vote determined the mayor who will appoint the people that run your child's school, fix your neighborhood roads, clear the snow promptly, would you vote?

Your vote matters. It matters in every election.

Voting is your time to speak. To not speak is to self-silence yourself.

Do you know who your district attorney, state attorney, and who your mayor are? Did you vote for all of them? How could you if you don't know them?

If you did not vote for the leader who appointed your police commissioner, you cannot hold him accountable when the police are not accountable. If the indictment of suspects becomes arbitrary in your neighborhood, you do not have a say because you probably do not know who your district or state attorney are.

Sometimes we unwittingly become the problem instead of a problem solver.

If you want to control a situation, the first step is to vote. If you really think about it, it is morally reprehensible to sit down and just complain about systemic laws when you don't vote for those you believe can bring about positive change.

Voting for the Office of the President of the United States alone cannot bring about the change you crave in your district, city, or state. Voting for the Office of the Governor of your state cannot bring about all the changes you desire in your district or city.

And continuously voting for a particular party and not holding them accountable is just a recipe for disaster. Your vote would be taken for granted by that party, while the other party won't even bother or care about you.

Today, most Americans don't have to risk their lives to participate in making changes that would right the injustices, especially systemic laws. Voting is just one—the easiest—way for all U.S. citizens, ages 18 to 108, to participate in the affairs of their communities and country. Use it.

There are those today who are still doing whatever they can to limit some eligible voters from voting. They understand the power of voting. They know that the only way you can change injustice is by changing those people who legislate the systemic laws that create discrimination, send more people to prisons, and take away the path to economic emancipation and other freedoms.

If you don't vote, you have given a free ride to creating more injustices. You have made it easier for the people, including yourself, to listen to comfortable lies instead of shaping your desires into reality.

Just voting is not enough either. You must hold your representatives accountable. You can write them and demand answers. You are the boss if you can vote and hold the elected accountable.

The opposing side would rather you did not vote, and they will go to any length to take your voting rights away. That is already happening in the United States. That in the United States, some are working toward limiting your abilities to vote is a pointer that they love the status quo.

They love the systemic racism.

They love that you and your people are incarcerated in high numbers. They love that you are prohibited from participating in this capitalism. They love it when you are traded on Wall Street like your grandfathers, but instead of the slave trade, you are traded as a prisoner.

Do not be a species with amnesia.

Take a look at your neighborhood schools, libraries, food markets, and water. Are they up to par with what is available in other communities? Perhaps the answer to the question is the reason why you must vote.

Do you like the incarceration rate in your neighborhood? Why is it higher than in other communities? This is where you must ask to know who your city attorney general is. It is the time to know who your borough president is. By the way, if you feel like talking to your representatives, you can easily do so face-to-face by booking an appointment.

You can influence who becomes your police commissioner when you vote for and hold your mayor accountable.

If you have an immigration problem or some other problem, you can ask to see your senator. Our senators do a great deal of good things outside of Washington, DC. Many constituents do not realize that they can call and speak with their senators and representatives.

People marched and made the ultimate sacrifice for every American to vote. Use your votes to right your situation.

Meanwhile, have you noticed that many poor young people—all peoples—think that segregation is no longer a big deal because a few rich people treat them nice?

They also think that because Barack Obama was elected the first black president, suddenly, racism has disappeared. Wake up. Don't be fooled.

Nothing has changed.

If it feels like change, it is because the media makes it seem that way. It's the same way the slogan—"land of the free"—has been bandied all over the world while incarcerating a whole group of people far more than other groups or countries do.

It's not the lies that should bother you. It is the insult to your intelligence that you should find offensive. If anything, the change is in the mastery and sophistication in the application of segregation laws.

In the end, the nonstop lamentation about economics and other deprivations won't solve the problems. It is only by voting, and always voting that you can put people who can do your bidding in positions to make policies.

The truth of the matter is that in the United States, we have become a country of people partly plagued by cognitive dissonance and hypocrisy. It is a pity that like mental slavery, those afflicted do not have the capability to be self-aware.

The United States of America is great. She was made great by certain laws and people. It is time to remove the badge of racism that pervades us. She can be greater.

She can be greater when she allows all her children to play in a level field. She can even be greatest when all her citizens are allowed to have a stake in America's capitalism, unhindered by any hidden barriers in the setup.

BIBLIOGRAPHY

Jaimes, M. A. (1992). *The State of America*. South End Press.

ONLINE RESOURCES:

Child Trends DataBank. (2007). *Family Structure*. Retrieved from http://www.childtrends.org/?indicators=family-structure

CivilWarTalk.com: (2012). *Freedmen, The Freed Slaves of the Civil War*. Retrieved from http://civilwartalk.com/threads/freedmen-the-freed-slaves-of-the-civil-war.77015/

Dictionary.com

Capitalism.org

Global Wealth Report. (2013). *Credit Suisse Global Wealth Databook*: 2013 report. Retrieved from http://images.smh.com.au/file/2013/10/09/4815797/cs_global_wealth_report_2013_WEB_low%2520pdf.pdf

http://legal-dictionary.thefreedictionary.com/Rule+of+law

Madison M. (2013). *Why Do Black People Always Vote Democratic?* Retrieved from http://thoughtcatalog.com/madison-moore/2013/05/why-do-black-people-always-vote-democratic/

Moore A. (2014). *8 Ways Racism Benefits All White People*. Retrieved from http://atlantablackstar.com/2014/09/17/8-ways-racism-benefits-all-white-people/4/

Moran Rick. (2015). *We're #20! U.S Sinks Again in Cato's Human Freedom Index*. Retrieved from http://pjmedia.com/tatler/2015/08/19/were-20-us-sinks-again-in-catos-human-freedom-index/

Reich, M. (1974). *Economics of Racism*. Retrieved from http://tomweston.net/ReichRacism.pdf

Reyes E.A. (2013). *Poor, mostly black areas face supermarket 'double jeopardy'* Retrieved from http://articles.latimes.com/2013/oct/30/science/la-sci-sn-poor-black-neighborhoods-supermarkets-20131029

Wagner P. (2012). *Incarceration is not an equal opportunity punishment*. Retrieved from http://www.prisonpolicy.org/articles/notequal.html

Wikipedia: https://en.wikipedia.org/wiki/Headright

Wolfers J. et al. (2015). *The Methodology: 1.5 Million Missing Black Men*. Retrieved from http://www.nytimes.com/2015/04/21/upshot/the-methodology-1-5-million-missing-black-men.html?src=twr

DIAGRAMS & GRAPH

Wagner Peter. (2012*). Data Source: Statistics as of June 30, 2010 and December 31, 2010 from Correctional Population in the United States and from U.S. Census Summary File 1*. Retrieved from http://bjs.ojp.usdoj.gov/content/pub/pdf/cpus10.pdf

Economic Research Service www.ers.usda.gov